M000313537

Not by Might—Not by Power: © 1974 by Deborah Lynn
   Friedman (ASCAP) / Sounds Write Productions
   (ASCAP). Lyrics by Debbie Friedman based on
   Zechariah 4:6. www.debbiefriedman.com
   and www.soundswrite.com

Or Zarua: Psalm 97:11

Oseh Shalom: Liturgy

Shir Chadash: Psalm 96:1

Shiru L'Adonai: Psalm 96:1–2

Shiru Shir: Based on Psalm 96:1

V'eizehu: *Pirkei Avot* 4:1

Wherever You Go: © 1983 by Laurence Elis Milder.
   Lyrics by Larry Milder.

Yad B'Yad: © 1987 by Sweet Louise Music. Lyrics by
   Craig Taubman based on *Pirkei Avot* 3:21.

Yism'chu HaShamayim: Psalm 96:11

Hatikvah—Israeli National Anthem: Naftali Imber

The Star-Spangled Banner—U.S. National Anthem:
   Francis Scott Key

O Canada—Canadian National Anthem: Robert Stanley
   Weir

בִּרְכּוֹן מִקְדָּשׁ מְעָט

Birkon Mikdash M'at

NFTY's Bencher

Jeremy Gimbel, Editor

A Joint Project of

in cooperation with the
Central Conference of American Rabbis

URJ Press is the publishing arm of the Union for Reform Judaism, serving Reform congregations in North America.

The North American Federation of Temple Youth (NFTY) is the Reform Jewish youth movement, uniting nearly 500 local synagogue youth groups.

The Central Conference of American Rabbis (CCAR) is the international rabbinic association of Reform Judaism.

Typesetting: El Ot Pre Press & Computing Ltd., Tel Aviv
This book is printed on acid-free paper.
Copyright © 2005 by URJ Press
Manufactured in the United States of America
10 9 8 7 6 5 4 3

▨ CONTENTS

Birkat HaMazon: Blessing after Eating

Z'mirot L'Shabbat: Songs for Shabbat

Z'mirot L'Chol Yom: Songs for Every Day

WORSHIP *ADONAI* WITH JOY.
Psalm 100:2

Birkon Mikdash M'at is a *bencher*—*bencher* is Yiddish and *birkon* is Hebrew—a small, portable book of songs, prayers, and blessings. *Benchers* have been used for generations, but this publication marks the first edition created by NFTY—the North American Federation of Temple Youth. In the future, *Birkon Mikdash M'at* may be changed to reflect the worship and ritual changes in the Reform Movement.

Throughout the Reform Movement—at camps, regional NFTY events, synagogue youth group meetings, and other times of gathering—prayers such as *Birkat HaMazon* and Shabbat blessings are recited and then followed by communal singing. *Birkon Mikdash M'at* is designed to facilitate and enhance the joy of singing in groups, the ritual moments of holiday observance, the spiritual experience of Shabbat.

I hope that *Birkon Mikdash M'at* will find its way into your events, your camps, and your daily Jewish life.

■ ACKNOWLEDGMENTS

It takes a village to raise a leader, and it took the assistance of an incredible group of people to make this project a reality.

I would first like to thank Matt Soffer for his one-on-one support, feedback, and encouragement. *Birkon Mikdash M'at* would have assumed a very different form if not for the supportive guidance and creative suggestions of Rabbi Dan Freelander, for which I am truly grateful. I would also like to express my thanks to Hope Chernak, Rabbi Eve Rudin, Rabbi Michael Friedman, Rabbi Andrew Davids, and Rabbi Sue Ann Wasserman for their assistance in reviewing and guiding the *bencher* from its earliest stages. Additionally, I would like to thank the 2004–05 NFTY board—Daniel Zadoff, David Silverstein, Mira Lyon, Justin Felder—and the Religious and Cultural VP network. Thanks are due to Kathy Parnass and the URJ production department for copyediting and designing the first edition of this document. I would especially like to thank Joel Eglash for helping us make great song choices. For their help in creating the second edition, I would also like to thank Debra Hirsch Corman, Ron Ghatan, Cantor Alane Katzew, Victor Ney, and Rabbi Hara Person. I would also like to thank Rabbi Elliot Stevens of the CCAR for giving us permission to use their material. Lastly, I extend a sincere thank you to the countless numbers who made comments and suggestions about the *bencher* in its various forms. To the village who raised this leader: *todah rabbah*.

L'shalom,

Jeremy Gimbel
NFTY Religious and Cultural VP 2004–05

▪ PERMISSIONS

Every attempt has been made to obtain permission to reprint previously published material. The publishers gratefully acknowledge the following for permission to reprint previously published material:

CRAIG TAUBMAN: *"Yad B'Yad"* Lyrics by Craig Taubman. © 1983 by Sweet Louise Music. Reprinted by permission of Craig Taubman.

DAN NICHOLS: *"B'Tzelem Elohim"* Lyrics by Dan Nichols and Mike Moskowitz. © 2001 by Dan Nichols. Reprinted by permission of Dan Nichols; *"Kehillah Kedoshah"* Lyrics by Dan Nichols and Mike Moskowitz. © 2002 by Dan Nichols. Reprinted by permission of Dan Nichols; *"L'takein* (The Na Na Song)" Lyrics by Ron Klotz. © 2001 by Dan Nichols. Reprinted by permission of Dan Nichols.

LARRY MILDER: "Wherever You Go" Lyrics by Larry Milder. © 1983 by Laurence Elis Milder. Reprinted by permission of Larry Milder.

SOUNDS WRITE PRODUCTIONS: "Not By Might— Not by Power" from *Not By Might–Not By Power*. Lyrics by Debbie Friedman. © 1974 by Deborah Lynn Friedman/ Sounds Write Productions. Reprinted by permission of Sounds Write Productions; "Miriam's Song" from *And You Shall Be a Blessing*. Lyrics by Debbie Friedman. © 1988 by Deborah Lynn Friedman/Sounds Write Productions. Reprinted by permission of Sounds Write Productions.

▣ *B'RACHOT L'SHABBAT:*
BLESSINGS FOR SHABBAT

BLESSINGS TO WELCOME SHABBAT

Giving *Tzedakah*

Our tradition invites each of us to give tzedakah
before the beginning of Shabbat. Consider placing
a tzedakah container near your Shabbat table, making
a contribution, and reciting this blessing.

בָּרוּךְ אַתָּה יְיָ, אֱלֹהֵינוּ מֶלֶךְ הָעוֹלָם,
אֲשֶׁר קִדְּשָׁנוּ בְּמִצְוֹתָיו וְצִוָּנוּ לִרְדוֹף צֶדֶק.

Baruch atah Adonai, Eloheinu Melech haolam,
asher kid'shanu b'mitzvotav v'tzivanu lirdof tzedek.

Blessed are You, Eternal our God, Sovereign of the
universe: You hallow us with Your mitzvot and
command us to pursue justice.

May we, together with all our people,
Respond to the needs of others.
From the fruits of our harvest this week,
We share with others.

And so we gain blessing:
Our lives have meaning,
Our lives have love.

As You greet us with Your angels on Shabbat,
May we be Your messengers to the world.

Shalom Aleichem

שָׁלוֹם עֲלֵיכֶם, מַלְאֲכֵי הַשָּׁרֵת, מַלְאֲכֵי עֶלְיוֹן,
מִמֶּלֶךְ מַלְכֵי הַמְּלָכִים, הַקָּדוֹשׁ בָּרוּךְ הוּא.

בּוֹאֲכֶם לְשָׁלוֹם, מַלְאֲכֵי הַשָּׁלוֹם, מַלְאֲכֵי עֶלְיוֹן,
מִמֶּלֶךְ מַלְכֵי הַמְּלָכִים, הַקָּדוֹשׁ בָּרוּךְ הוּא.

בָּרְכוּנִי לְשָׁלוֹם, מַלְאֲכֵי הַשָּׁלוֹם, מַלְאֲכֵי עֶלְיוֹן,
מִמֶּלֶךְ מַלְכֵי הַמְּלָכִים, הַקָּדוֹשׁ בָּרוּךְ הוּא.

צֵאתְכֶם לְשָׁלוֹם, מַלְאֲכֵי הַשָּׁלוֹם, מַלְאֲכֵי עֶלְיוֹן,
מִמֶּלֶךְ מַלְכֵי הַמְּלָכִים, הַקָּדוֹשׁ בָּרוּךְ הוּא.

*Shalom aleichem, malachei hashareit, malachei Elyon,
miMelech malchei ham'lachim, HaKadosh baruch hu.*

*Bo-achem l'shalom, malachei hashalom, malachei Elyon,
miMelech malchei ham'lachim, HaKadosh baruch hu.*

*Bar'chuni l'shalom, malachei hashalom, malachei Elyon,
miMelech malchei ham'lachim, haKadosh baruch hu.*

*Tzeit'chem l'shalom, malachei hashalom, malachei Elyon,
miMelech malchei ham'lachim, haKadosh baruch hu.*

Peace be to you, O ministering angels, messengers of the
Most High, Majesty of majesties, Holy One of Blessing.

Enter in peace, O messengers of peace, angels of the Most
High, Majesty of majesties, Holy One of Blessing.

Bless me with peace, O messengers of peace, angels of the
Most High, Majesty of majesties, Holy One of Blessing.

Depart in peace, O messengers of peace, angels of the
Most High, Majesty of majesties, Holy One of Blessing.

Lighting Shabbat Candles

The candles are lit before this blessing is recited.

בָּרוּךְ אַתָּה יְיָ, אֱלֹהֵינוּ מֶלֶךְ הָעוֹלָם,
אֲשֶׁר קִדְּשָׁנוּ בְּמִצְוֹתָיו וְצִוָּנוּ לְהַדְלִיק נֵר שֶׁל שַׁבָּת.

Baruch atah Adonai, Eloheinu Melech haolam,
asher kid'shanu b'mitzvotav v'tzivanu
l'hadlik ner shel Shabbat.

Blessed are You, Eternal our God, Sovereign of time
and space. You hallow us with Your mitzvot and
command us to kindle the lights of Shabbat.

Blessings for Loved Ones

In Praise of a Woman

A woman of valor, seek her out;
she is to be valued above rubies.
She opens her hand to those in need
and extends her help to the poor.
Adorned with strength and dignity,
she faces the future cheerfully.
Her speech is wise; the law of kindness is on her lips.
Those who love her rise up with praise and call her blessed:
"Many have done well, but you surpass them all."
Charm is deceptive and beauty short-lived,
but a woman loyal to God has truly earned praise.
Honor her for all of her offerings;
her life proclaims her praise.

Adapted from Proverbs 31

In Praise of a Man

A house is built by wisdom,
and is established by understanding;
by knowledge are its rooms filled
with all precious and beautiful things.

O God, who will stay in Your tent,
who may dwell on Your holy mountain?
One who lives without blame,
and who does what is right,
whose heart acknowledges the truth;
whose tongue is not given to slander;
who has never done harm to his fellow.

One who acts thus shall never be shaken.

A wise man is strength.

Adapted from Proverbs 24:3–5, Psalm 15

For a Child

Blessed is the parent and blessed is the child
when our hearts are turned toward one another.
Blessed is the home filled with laughter and light,
and joyful spirit of Shabbat.
Blessed is the home when, even in difficult times,
we can fill it with the light of Shabbat.

Tonight I remind you:
Seek truth always.
Speak words of kindness.
Be just and loving in your deeds.
Let Torah be your guide.

A noble heritage has been entrusted to you; guard it well.

May God bless you and protect you.

For a boy	**For a girl**

יְשִׂמְךָ אֱלֹהִים
כְּאֶפְרַיִם וְכִמְנַשֶּׁה.

יְשִׂמֵךְ אֱלֹהִים
כְּשָׂרָה, רִבְקָה, רָחֵל וְלֵאָה.

Y'sim'cha Elohim	*Y'simeich Elohim*
k'Efrayim v'chiM'nasheh.	*k'Sarah, Rivkah, Racheil, v'Lei-ah.*
May God inspire you to live	May God inspire you to live
like Ephraim and Manasseh.	like Sarah, Rebekah, Rachel, and Leah.

For both boys and girls

יְבָרֶכְךָ יְהֹוָה וְיִשְׁמְרֶךָ.
יָאֵר יְהֹוָה פָּנָיו אֵלֶיךָ וִיחֻנֶּךָּ.
יִשָּׂא יְהֹוָה פָּנָיו אֵלֶיךָ וְיָשֵׂם לְךָ שָׁלוֹם.

Y'varech'cha Adonai v'yishm'recha.
Ya-eir Adonai panav eilecha vichuneka.
Yisa Adonai panav eilecha v'yaseim l'cha shalom.

May God bless you and keep you.
May God's light shine upon you, and may God be
gracious to you.
May you feel God's Presence within you always, and may
you find peace.

Kiddush for **Shabbat** Evening

Raise a Kiddush *cup with wine or grape juice
(both are "fruit of the vine"), and recite:*

"Six days you shall labor and do all your work, but the
seventh day is a Sabbath of the Eternal your God." With
the fruit of the vine, our symbol of joy, we celebrate this
sacred day, on which cares and sorrows fade from our
minds. We give thanks for life and its blessings, for work

and rest, for home and love and friendship. On Shabbat, eternal sign of Creation, we rejoice that we are created in the image of God.

Some continue here, others on the next page.

וַיְהִי עֶרֶב וַיְהִי בֹקֶר יוֹם הַשִּׁשִּׁי.

Vay'hi erev vay'hi voker yom hashishi.

And there was evening and there was morning, the sixth day.

וַיְכֻלּוּ הַשָּׁמַיִם וְהָאָרֶץ וְכָל־צְבָאָם. וַיְכַל אֱלֹהִים בַּיּוֹם הַשְּׁבִיעִי מְלַאכְתּוֹ אֲשֶׁר עָשָׂה. וַיִּשְׁבֹּת בַּיּוֹם הַשְּׁבִיעִי מִכָּל־מְלַאכְתּוֹ אֲשֶׁר עָשָׂה. וַיְבָרֶךְ אֱלֹהִים אֶת־יוֹם הַשְּׁבִיעִי וַיְקַדֵּשׁ אֹתוֹ כִּי בוֹ שָׁבַת מִכָּל־מְלַאכְתּוֹ אֲשֶׁר בָּרָא אֱלֹהִים לַעֲשׂוֹת.

Vay'chulu hashamayim v'haaretz v'chol tz'vaam.
Vay'chal Elohim bayom hash'vi-i m'lachto asher asah.
Vayishbot bayom hash'vi-i mikol m'lachto asher asah.
Vay'varech Elohim et yom hash'vi-i vay'kadeish oto,
ki vo shavat mikol m'lachto asher bara Elohim laasot.

Now the whole universe—sky, earth, and all their array— was completed. With the seventh day God ended the work of creation, resting on the seventh day, with all the work completed. Then God blessed the seventh day and sanctified it, this day having completed the work of creation.

בָּרוּךְ אַתָּה יְיָ, אֱלֹהֵינוּ מֶלֶךְ הָעוֹלָם, בּוֹרֵא פְּרִי הַגָּפֶן.
בָּרוּךְ אַתָּה יְיָ, אֱלֹהֵינוּ מֶלֶךְ הָעוֹלָם, אֲשֶׁר קִדְּשָׁנוּ
בְּמִצְוֹתָיו וְרָצָה בָנוּ, וְשַׁבַּת קָדְשׁוֹ בְּאַהֲבָה וּבְרָצוֹן
הִנְחִילָנוּ, זִכָּרוֹן לְמַעֲשֵׂה בְרֵאשִׁית. כִּי הוּא יוֹם
תְּחִלָּה לְמִקְרָאֵי קֹדֶשׁ, זֵכֶר לִיצִיאַת מִצְרָיִם. כִּי בָנוּ
בָחַרְתָּ, וְאוֹתָנוּ קִדַּשְׁתָּ, מִכָּל הָעַמִּים. וְשַׁבַּת קָדְשְׁךָ
בְּאַהֲבָה וּבְרָצוֹן הִנְחַלְתָּנוּ. בָּרוּךְ אַתָּה יְיָ, מְקַדֵּשׁ
הַשַּׁבָּת.

Baruch atah Adonai, Eloheinu Melech haolam,
borei p'ri hagafen.
Baruch atah Adonai, Eloheinu Melech haolam,
asher kid'shanu b'mitzvotav v'ratzah vanu,
v'Shabbat kodsho b'ahavah uv'ratzon hinchilanu,
zikaron l'maaseih v'reishit.
Ki hu yom t'chilah l'mikra-ei kodesh,
zeicher litziat Mitzrayim.
Ki vanu vacharta, v'otanu kidashta, mikol haamim.
V'Shabbat kodsh'cha b'ahavah uv'ratzon hinchaltanu.
Baruch atah Adonai, m'kadeish haShabbat.

Praise to You, Eternal our God, Sovereign of the
Universe, Creator of the fruit of the vine. Praise to You,
Eternal our God, Sovereign of the universe, who sanctifies
us with mitzvot and takes delight in us. In love and favor,
God made the holy Shabbat, our heritage as a reminder of
the work of Creation. It is first among our sacred days,
and a remembrance of the Exodus from Egypt. O God,
You have chosen us and set us apart from all the peoples,
and in love and favor have given us the Sabbath day as a
sacred inheritance. Praise to You, Eternal, for the Sabbath
and its holiness.

Washing Hands

See page 21 for this blessing.

Blessing for Challah

Tradition invites us to have a challah on our table, covered with a cloth. Some have two challot on the table to symbolize the double portion of manna the Israelites received in the Sinai Desert every Friday (Exodus 16:11–30). Remove the cover and recite:

בָּרוּךְ אַתָּה יְיָ, אֱלֹהֵינוּ מֶלֶךְ הָעוֹלָם,
הַמּוֹצִיא לֶחֶם מִן הָאָרֶץ.

*Baruch atah Adonai, Eloheinu Melech haolam,
hamotzi lechem min haaretz.*

Our praise to You, Eternal our God, Sovereign of the universe, who brings forth bread from the earth.

Birkat HaMazon: Blessing after Eating

See page 24 (short version) or 30 (long version).

KIDDUSH FOR SHABBAT MORNING

וְשָׁמְרוּ בְנֵי יִשְׂרָאֵל אֶת הַשַּׁבָּת, לַעֲשׂוֹת אֶת הַשַּׁבָּת
לְדֹרֹתָם בְּרִית עוֹלָם. בֵּינִי וּבֵין בְּנֵי יִשְׂרָאֵל אוֹת הִיא
לְעֹלָם, כִּי שֵׁשֶׁת יָמִים עָשָׂה יְיָ אֶת הַשָּׁמַיִם וְאֶת
הָאָרֶץ, וּבַיּוֹם הַשְּׁבִיעִי שָׁבַת וַיִּנָּפַשׁ.

V'sham'ru v'nei Yisrael et haShabbat,
laasot et haShabbat l'dorotam b'rit olam.
Beini uvein b'nei Yisrael ot hi l'olam,
ki sheishet yamim asah Adonai et hashamayim v'et haaretz,
uvayom hash'vi-i shavat vayinafash.

The people of Israel shall keep the Sabbath, observing
the Sabbath in every generation for all time. It is a sign
forever between Me and the people of Israel, for in six
days the Eternal God made heaven and earth, and on
the seventh day, God rested from all labor.

עַל־כֵּן בֵּרַךְ יְיָ אֶת־יוֹם הַשַּׁבָּת וַיְקַדְּשֵׁהוּ.

Al kein beirach Adonai et yom haShabbat vay'kad'sheihu.

Thus the Eternal blessed the seventh day and called
it holy.

בָּרוּךְ אַתָּה יְיָ, אֱלֹהֵינוּ מֶלֶךְ הָעוֹלָם, בּוֹרֵא פְּרִי הַגָּפֶן.

Baruch atah Adonai, Eloheinu Melech haolam,
borei p'ri hagafen.

Blessed are You, Eternal our God, Sovereign of the
universe, Creator of the fruit of the vine.

HAVDALAH

As Shabbat ends, the Havdalah *candle is lit. It is customary to raise the cup of wine or grape juice high when the last sentence is recited and then proceed to the blessing.*

הִנֵּה אֵל יְשׁוּעָתִי, אֶבְטַח וְלֹא אֶפְחָד. כִּי עָזִּי וְזִמְרָת יָהּ יְהֹוָה, וַיְהִי לִי לִישׁוּעָה. וּשְׁאַבְתֶּם מַיִם בְּשָׂשׂוֹן מִמַּעַיְנֵי הַיְשׁוּעָה. לַיהֹוָה הַיְשׁוּעָה, עַל עַמְּךָ בִרְכָתֶךָ, סֶּלָה. יְהֹוָה צְבָאוֹת עִמָּנוּ, מִשְׂגָּב לָנוּ אֱלֹהֵי יַעֲקֹב, סֶלָה. יְהֹוָה צְבָאוֹת, אַשְׁרֵי אָדָם בֹּטֵחַ בָּךְ! יְהֹוָה הוֹשִׁיעָה; הַמֶּלֶךְ יַעֲנֵנוּ בְיוֹם קָרְאֵנוּ. לַיְּהוּדִים הָיְתָה אוֹרָה וְשִׂמְחָה וְשָׂשֹׂן וִיקָר; כֵּן תִּהְיֶה לָּנוּ. כּוֹס יְשׁוּעוֹת אֶשָּׂא, וּבְשֵׁם יְהֹוָה אֶקְרָא.

Hineih El y'shuati, evtach v'lo efchad.
Ki ozi v'zimrat Yah Adonai, vay'hi li lishuah.
Ush'avtem mayim b'sason mimaay'nei hay'shuah.
L'Adonai hay'shuah, al am'cha virchatecha, selah.
Adonai tz'vaot imanu, misgav lanu Elohei Yaakov, selah.
Adonai tz'vaot, ashrei adam botei-ach bach!
Adonai hoshiah; haMelech yaaneinu v'yom koreinu.
LaY'hudim hay'tah orah v'simchah v'sason vikar;
kein tihyeh lanu.
Kos y'shuot esa, uv'shem Adonai ekra.

Behold, God is my help; trusting in the Eternal One, I am not afraid. For the Eternal One is my strength and my song, and has become my salvation. With joy we draw water from the wells of salvation. The Eternal One brings deliverance and blessing to the people. The God of the hosts of heaven is with us; the God of Jacob is our stronghold. God of the hosts of heaven, happy is the one who trusts in You! Save us, Eternal One; answer us, when we call upon You. Give us light and joy, gladness and honor, as in the happiest days of our people's past. Then shall we lift up the cup to rejoice in Your saving power, and call out Your name in praise.

Lift the cup of wine or grape juice, and recite the blessing:

בָּרוּךְ אַתָּה יְיָ, אֱלֹהֵינוּ מֶלֶךְ הָעוֹלָם, בּוֹרֵא פְּרִי הַגָּפֶן.

Baruch atah Adonai, Eloheinu Melech haolam,
borei p'ri hagafen.

We praise You, Eternal God, Sovereign of the universe, Creator of the fruit of the vine.

Hold up the spice box, and recite the blessing:

בָּרוּךְ אַתָּה יְיָ, אֱלֹהֵינוּ מֶלֶךְ הָעוֹלָם, בּוֹרֵא מִינֵי בְשָׂמִים.

Baruch atah Adonai, Eloheinu Melech haolam,
borei minei v'samim.

We praise You, Eternal God, Sovereign of the universe, Creator of all spices.

Circulate the spice box so that all can inhale its fragrance.

Lift the Havdalah *candle, and recite the blessing:*

בָּרוּךְ אַתָּה יְיָ, אֱלֹהֵינוּ מֶלֶךְ הָעוֹלָם,
בּוֹרֵא מְאוֹרֵי הָאֵשׁ.

Baruch atah Adonai, Eloheinu Melech haolam,
borei m'orei ha-eish.

We praise You, Eternal God, Sovereign of the universe,
Creator of fire.

Some follow the custom of looking at the reflection
of the light on fingernails and the shadows created
by the light.

Hold the Havdalah *candle, and recite the blessing:*

בָּרוּךְ אַתָּה יְיָ, אֱלֹהֵינוּ מֶלֶךְ הָעוֹלָם, הַמַּבְדִּיל בֵּין
קֹדֶשׁ לְחוֹל, בֵּין אוֹר לְחֹשֶׁךְ, בֵּין יִשְׂרָאֵל לָעַמִּים, בֵּין
יוֹם הַשְּׁבִיעִי לְשֵׁשֶׁת יְמֵי הַמַּעֲשֶׂה. בָּרוּךְ אַתָּה יְיָ,
הַמַּבְדִּיל בֵּין קֹדֶשׁ לְחוֹל.

Baruch atah Adonai, Eloheinu Melech haolam,
hamavdil bein kodesh l'chol, bein or l'choshech,
bein Yisrael laamim,
bein yom hash'vi-i l'sheishet y'mei hamaaseh.
Baruch atah Adonai, hamavdil bein kodesh l'chol.

We praise You, Eternal God, Sovereign of the universe:
You distinguish the commonplace from the holy; You create
light and darkness, Israel and the nations, the seventh day
of rest and the six days of labor. We praise You, O God:
You call us to distinguish the commonplace from the holy.

Sip the wine or grape juice, and sing:

הַמַּבְדִּיל בֵּין־קֹדֶשׁ לְחֹל, חַטֹּאתֵינוּ הוּא יִמְחֹל,
זַרְעֵנוּ וְכַסְפֵּנוּ יַרְבֶּה כַחוֹל, וְכַכּוֹכָבִים בַּלָּיְלָה.

Hamavdil bein kodesh l'chol, chatoteinu hu yimchol,
zareinu v'chaspeinu yarbeh kachol, v'chakochavim balailah.

May the One who distinguished the holy from the
profane forgive us when we err in our ways. May our
children and prosperity increase like the sands on the
shore and the stars in the night.

Extinguish the candle in wine, and sing:

אֵלִיָּֽהוּ הַנָּבִיא, אֵלִיָּֽהוּ הַתִּשְׁבִּי, אֵלִיָּֽהוּ הַגִּלְעָדִי.
בִּמְהֵרָה בְיָמֵינוּ, יָבוֹא אֵלֵינוּ, עִם מָשִׁיחַ בֶּן־דָּוִד.

Eliyahu HaNavi, Eliyahu HaTishbi, Eliyahu HaGiladi.
Bimheirah v'yameinu, yavo eileinu, im Mashiach ben David.

Elijah the prophet, the Tishbite, the Gileadite: come
to us soon, to herald our redemption.

B'RACHOT L'CHAGIM:
BLESSINGS FOR HOLIDAYS

LIGHTING HOLIDAY CANDLES

May these Festival lights open our eyes to the joys in life.
We are blessed with so much:
food enough to sustain us,
beauty that delights the eye,
the freedom to be ourselves,
the knowledge of Torah that shapes our moral being,
the heritage of celebration that unites us as a people.
Praised be our God, for life, for sustenance, and for this
    festive day.

Light the candles, and recite these blessings:

בָּרוּךְ אַתָּה יְיָ, אֱלֹהֵינוּ מֶלֶךְ הָעוֹלָם, אֲשֶׁר קִדְּשָׁנוּ
בְּמִצְוֹתָיו וְצִוָּנוּ לְהַדְלִיק נֵר [שֶׁל שַׁבָּת וְ]שֶׁל יוֹם טוֹב.

Baruch atah Adonai, Eloheinu Melech haolam,
asher kid'shanu b'mitzvotav v'tzivanu
l'hadlik ner (shel Shabbat v') shel Yom Tov.

Blessed are You, Eternal our God, Sovereign of time and
space. You hallow us with Your mitzvot and command us
to kindle the lights of (Shabbat and) this sacred occasion.

בָּרוּךְ אַתָּה יְיָ, אֱלֹהֵינוּ מֶלֶךְ הָעוֹלָם,
שֶׁהֶחֱיָנוּ וְקִיְּמָנוּ וְהִגִּיעָנוּ לַזְּמַן הַזֶּה.

Baruch atah Adonai, Eloheinu Melech haolam,
shehecheyanu v'kiy'manu, v'higianu laz'man hazeh.

Praise to You, Eternal our God, Sovereign of the universe,
for giving us life, sustaining us, and enabling us to reach
this season.

Kiddush for Holidays

Raise a Kiddush *cup with wine or grape juice*
(both are "fruit of the vine") and recite:

בָּרוּךְ אַתָּה יְיָ אֱלֹהֵינוּ מֶלֶךְ הָעוֹלָם, בּוֹרֵא פְּרִי הַגָּפֶן.
בָּרוּךְ אַתָּה יְיָ אֱלֹהֵינוּ מֶלֶךְ הָעוֹלָם אֲשֶׁר בָּחַר־בָּנוּ
מִכָּל־עָם וְרוֹמְמָנוּ מִכָּל־לָשׁוֹן וְקִדְּשָׁנוּ בְּמִצְוֹתָיו.
וַתִּתֶּן־לָנוּ יְיָ אֱלֹהֵינוּ בְּאַהֲבָה (שַׁבָּתוֹת לִמְנוּחָה וּ)
מוֹעֲדִים לְשִׂמְחָה חַגִּים וּזְמַנִּים לְשָׂשׂוֹן אֶת־יוֹם
(הַשַּׁבָּת הַזֶּה וְאֶת־יוֹם)

• חַג הַמַּצּוֹת הַזֶּה זְמַן חֵרוּתֵנוּ
• חַג הַשָּׁבֻעוֹת הַזֶּה זְמַן מַתַּן תּוֹרָתֵנוּ
• חַג הַסֻּכּוֹת הַזֶּה זְמַן שִׂמְחָתֵנוּ
• הַשְּׁמִינִי חַג הָעֲצֶרֶת הַזֶּה זְמַן שִׂמְחָתֵנוּ

מִקְרָא קֹדֶשׁ זֵכֶר לִיצִיאַת מִצְרָיִם. כִּי בָנוּ בָחַרְתָּ
וְאוֹתָנוּ קִדַּשְׁתָּ מִכָּל־הָעַמִּים (וְשַׁבָּת) וּמוֹעֲדֵי קָדְשֶׁךָ
(בְּאַהֲבָה וּבְרָצוֹן) בְּשִׂמְחָה וּבְשָׂשׂוֹן הִנְחַלְתָּנוּ.
בָּרוּךְ אַתָּה יְיָ מְקַדֵּשׁ (הַשַּׁבָּת וְ) יִשְׂרָאֵל וְהַזְּמַנִּים.

Baruch atah Adonai Eloheinu Melech haolam
borei p'ri hagafen.
Baruch atah Adonai Eloheinu melech haolam
asher bachar banu mikol am, v'rom'manu mikol lashon,
v'kid'shanu b'mitzvotav.
Vatiten lanu Adonai Eloheinu b'ahavah
(Shabatot lim'nuchah u) mo'adim l'simchah,
chagim uz'manim l'sason et yom (haShabbat hazeh v'et yom)
   Chag hamatzot hazeh—z'man cheiruteinu
   Chag haShavuot hazeh—z'man matan Torateinu
   Chag haSukkot hazeh—z'man simchateinu
   HaSh'mini chag haAtzeret hazeh—z'man simchateinu
mikra kodesh, zeicher litzi'at Mitzrayim.
Ki vanu vacharta,
v'otanu kidashta mikol haamim
(v'Shabbat) umo-adei kodsh'cha
(b'ahavah uv'ratzon) b'simchah uv'sason hinchaltanu.
Baruch atah Adonai
m'kadeish (haShabbat v') Yisrael v'haz'manim.

Praise to You, Eternal our God, Sovereign of the universe,
Creator of the fruit of the vine. Praise to You, Eternal our
God, Sovereign of the universe, who has chosen us from
among the peoples, exalting us by hallowing us with
mitzvot. In Your love, Eternal our God, You have given
us (Sabbaths of rest,) feasts of gladness, and seasons of joy:
this (Sabbath day and this) Festival of
   Pesach—season of our freedom;
   Shavuot—season of revelation;
   Sukkot—season of our gladness;
   Atzeret-Simchat Torah—season of our gladness;
to unite in worship and recall the Exodus from Egypt.
For You have chosen us from all the peoples, consecrating

us to Your service, and giving us (the Sabbath, a sign of Your love and favor, and) the Festivals, a time of gladness and joy. Praise to You, Eternal, who sanctifies (the Sabbath,) the House of Israel and the Festivals.

LIGHTING THE CHANUKAH CANDLES

עַל הַנִּסִּים, וְעַל הַפֻּרְקָן, וְעַל הַגְּבוּרוֹת,
וְעַל הַתְּשׁוּעוֹת, וְעַל הַמִּלְחָמוֹת, שֶׁעָשִׂיתָ לַדּוֹרוֹתֵינוּ,
בַּיָּמִים הָהֵם בַּזְּמַן הַזֶּה.

Al hanisim, v'al hapurkan,
v'al hag'vurot, v'al hat'shuot, v'al hamilchamot,
she-asita l'doroteinu, bayamim haheim baz'man hazeh.

We give thanks for the redeeming wonders and mighty deeds by which, at this season, our people was saved in days of old.

Place one new candle in the chanukiyah *for each night of Chanukah, increasing one candle per night (plus the* shamash). *Olive oil may be used. Candles should be placed from right to left. Light the* shamash *first, recite the blessings, and use the* shamash *to light the candles from from the left to the right.*

בָּרוּךְ אַתָּה יְיָ, אֱלֹהֵינוּ מֶלֶךְ הָעוֹלָם,
אֲשֶׁר קִדְּשָׁנוּ בְּמִצְוֹתָיו וְצִוָּנוּ לְהַדְלִיק נֵר שֶׁל חֲנֻכָּה.

Baruch atah Adonai, Eloheinu Melech haolam,
asher kid'shanu b'mitzvotav v'tzivanu
l'hadlik ner shel Chanukah.

Blessed are You, Eternal our God, Sovereign of all,
who hallows us with mitzvot and commands us to kindle
the Chanukah lights.

בָּרוּךְ אַתָּה יְיָ, אֱלֹהֵינוּ מֶלֶךְ הָעוֹלָם,
שֶׁעָשָׂה נִסִּים לְדוֹרוֹתֵינוּ בַּיָּמִים הָהֵם בַּזְּמַן הַזֶּה.

Baruch atah Adonai, Eloheinu Melech haolam,
she-asah nisim l'doroteinu bayamim haheim baz'man hazeh.

Blessed are You, Eternal our God, Sovereign of all,
who performed wondrous deeds for our ancestors in days
of old at this season.

On the first night only

בָּרוּךְ אַתָּה יְיָ, אֱלֹהֵינוּ מֶלֶךְ הָעוֹלָם,
שֶׁהֶחֱיָנוּ וְקִיְּמָנוּ וְהִגִּיעָנוּ לַזְּמַן הַזֶּה.

Baruch atah Adonai, Eloheinu Melech haolam,
shehecheyanu v'kiy'manu v'higianu laz'man hazeh.

Blessed are You, Eternal our God, Sovereign of all,
for giving us life, for sustaining us, and for enabling us
to reach this season.

BLESSINGS FOR SUKKOT

Blessing for Dwelling in the Sukkah

It is a mitzvah to celebrate in the sukkah. While the Torah instructs us to live in the sukkah for seven days, many choose to only have meals in the sukkah. When eating or reciting Kiddush *in the sukkah, recite this blessing:*

בָּרוּךְ אַתָּה יְיָ, אֱלֹהֵינוּ מֶלֶךְ הָעוֹלָם,
אֲשֶׁר קִדְּשָׁנוּ בְּמִצְוֹתָיו וְצִוָּנוּ לֵישֵׁב בַּסֻּכָּה.

*Baruch atah Adonai, Eloheinu Melech haolam,
asher kid'shanu b'mitzvotav v'tzivanu leisheiv basukkah.*

Our praise to You, Eternal God, Sovereign of all:
You hallow us with Your mitzvot and command us to dwell in the sukkah.

Blessings for the *Lulav*

The lulav *is held up in the right hand, and the* etrog *is held* pitom *end (pointy side) down in the left hand. Facing east, recite the blessing. Then turn the* etrog *up and shake the entire bundle three times in each of six directions: straight ahead, right, back, left, up, and down.*

בָּרוּךְ אַתָּה יְיָ, אֱלֹהֵינוּ מֶלֶךְ הָעוֹלָם,
אֲשֶׁר קִדְּשָׁנוּ בְּמִצְוֹתָיו וְצִוָּנוּ עַל נְטִילַת לוּלָב.

*Baruch atah Adonai, Eloheinu Melech haolam,
asher kid'shanu b'mizvotav v'tzivanu al n'tilat lulav.*

Our praise to You, Eternal God, Sovereign of all,
whose mitzvot teach us holiness and who instructs us
to take up the *lulav*.

The first time you wave the *lulav* each year

בָּרוּךְ אַתָּה יְיָ, אֱלֹהֵינוּ מֶלֶךְ הָעוֹלָם,
שֶׁהֶחֱיָנוּ וְקִיְּמָנוּ וְהִגִּיעָנוּ לַזְּמַן הַזֶּה.

Baruch atah Adonai, Eloheinu Melech haolam,
shehecheyanu v'kiy'manu, v'higianu laz'man hazeh.

Our praise to You, Eternal God, Sovereign of all, who has
kept us alive, sustained us, and brought us to this season.

LIGHTING A *YAHRZEIT* (MEMORIAL) CANDLE

Before lighting a yahrzeit candle, take a moment to
bring to mind the relative you are remembering.
You might choose to read the following prayer:

O God, grant us strength as we mourn the loss of ____ .
We will always have cherished memories of him/her.
Bless our family with light and peace. May ____'s memory
continue to serve as a blessing and an inspiration to all
who knew and loved him/her.

Zichrono/zichronah livrachah.　　　זִכְרוֹנוֹ/זִכְרוֹנָהּ לִבְרָכָה.
His/her memory is a blessing.

Mourner's Kaddish may be recited at this time.

▣ *BIRCHOT HANEHENIN:* BLESSINGS FOR ENJOYMENT

WASHING HANDS

*It is customary to remove all jewelry from the hands
before washing. Fill a cup of water and pour it over your
right hand. (Note: If your dominant hand is your left
hand, reverse these instructions.) Next, take the cup in
your right hand and pour it over the left hand. This is
repeated two or three times. Then say the following
blessing before drying your hands. Some do not speak
between the hand-washing blessing and the blessing
over food.*

בָּרוּךְ אַתָּה יְיָ, אֱלֹהֵינוּ מֶלֶךְ הָעוֹלָם,
אֲשֶׁר קִדְּשָׁנוּ בְּמִצְוֹתָיו וְצִוָּנוּ עַל נְטִילַת יָדָיִם.

*Baruch atah Adonai, Eloheinu Melech haolam,
asher kid'shanu b'mitzvotav v'tzivanu al n'tilat yadayim.*

Our praise to You, Eternal our God, Sovereign of
the universe: You hallow us with Your mitzvot and
command us to lift up our hands.

EATING BREAD

בָּרוּךְ אַתָּה יְיָ, אֱלֹהֵינוּ מֶלֶךְ הָעוֹלָם,
הַמּוֹצִיא לֶחֶם מִן הָאָרֶץ.

*Baruch atah Adonai, Eloheinu Melech haolam,
hamotzi lechem min haaretz.*

Our praise to You, Eternal our God, Sovereign of the
universe, who brings forth bread from the earth.

EATING FOOD PREPARED FROM GRAIN (OTHER THAN BREAD)

בָּרוּךְ אַתָּה יְיָ, אֱלֹהֵינוּ מֶלֶךְ הָעוֹלָם,
בּוֹרֵא מִינֵי מְזוֹנוֹת.

Baruch atah Adonai, Eloheinu Melech haolam,
borei minei m'zonot.

Our praise to You, Eternal God, Sovereign of the universe, Creator of many kinds of food.

DRINKING WINE/GRAPE JUICE

בָּרוּךְ אַתָּה יְיָ, אֱלֹהֵינוּ מֶלֶךְ הָעוֹלָם, בּוֹרֵא פְּרִי הַגָּפֶן.

Baruch atah Adonai, Eloheinu Melech haolam,
borei p'ri hagafen.

Our praise to You, Eternal our God, Sovereign of the universe, Creator of the fruit of the vine.

EATING FRUIT

בָּרוּךְ אַתָּה יְיָ, אֱלֹהֵינוּ מֶלֶךְ הָעוֹלָם, בּוֹרֵא פְּרִי הָעֵץ.

Baruch atah Adonai, Eloheinu Melech haolam,
borei p'ri ha-eitz.

Our praise to You, Eternal our God, Sovereign of the universe, Creator of the fruit of the tree.

EATING FOOD THAT GROWS FROM THE GROUND

בָּרוּךְ אַתָּה יְיָ, אֱלֹהֵינוּ מֶלֶךְ הָעוֹלָם,
בּוֹרֵא פְּרִי הָאֲדָמָה.

Baruch atah Adonai, Eloheinu Melech haolam,
borei p'ri haadamah.

Our praise to You, Eternal our God, Sovereign of the
universe, Creator of the fruit of the earth.

ALL OTHER FOOD AND DRINK

בָּרוּךְ אַתָּה יְיָ, אֱלֹהֵינוּ מֶלֶךְ הָעוֹלָם,
שֶׁהַכֹּל נִהְיֶה בִּדְבָרוֹ.

Baruch atah Adonai, Eloheinu Melech haolam,
shehakol nihyeh bidvaro.

Our praise to You, Eternal our God, Sovereign of the
universe, at whose word all things come into being.

On Shabbat (from Psalm 126)

שִׁיר הַמַּעֲלוֹת, בְּשׁוּב יְהֹוָה אֶת־שִׁיבַת צִיּוֹן, הָיִינוּ
כְּחֹלְמִים. אָז יִמָּלֵא שְׂחוֹק פִּינוּ, וּלְשׁוֹנֵנוּ רִנָּה. אָז
יֹאמְרוּ בַגּוֹיִם: הִגְדִּיל יְהֹוָה לַעֲשׂוֹת עִם־אֵלֶּה. הִגְדִּיל
יְהֹוָה לַעֲשׂוֹת עִמָּנוּ, הָיִינוּ שְׂמֵחִים. שׁוּבָה יְהֹוָה
אֶת־שְׁבִיתֵנוּ כַּאֲפִיקִים בַּנֶּגֶב. הַזֹּרְעִים בְּדִמְעָה בְּרִנָּה
יִקְצֹרוּ. הָלוֹךְ יֵלֵךְ וּבָכֹה, נֹשֵׂא מֶשֶׁךְ־הַזָּרַע, בֹּא־יָבוֹא
בְרִנָּה, נֹשֵׂא אֲלֻמֹּתָיו.

Shir hamaalot,
b'shuv Adonai et shivat Tziyon hayinu k'chol'mim.
Az yimalei s'chok pinu, ul'shoneinu rinah.
Az yom'ru vagoyim: Higdil Adonai laasot im eileh.
Higdil Adonai laasot imanu, hayinu s'meichim.
Shuvah Adonai et sh'viteinu kaafikim baNegev.
Hazor'im b'dimah b'rinah yiktzoru.
Haloch yeileich uvachoh, nosei meshech hazara,
bo yavo v'rinah, nosei alumotav.

A pilgrim song. When God restored the exiles to Zion it
seemed like a dream. Our mouths were filled with laughter,
our tongues with joyful song. Then they said among the
nations: "God has done great things for them." Yes, God
is doing great things for us, and we are joyful. Restore
our fortunes, O God, as streams revive the desert. Then
those who have sown in tears shall reap in joy. Those who
go forth weeping, carrying bags of seeds, shall come home
with shouts of joy, bearing their sheaves.

If there are fewer than three people reciting Birkat HaMazon *together, skip this first section and continue in the middle of page 26.*

Leader

חֲבֵרַי נְבָרֵךְ!

Chaveirai n'vareich!

Let us praise God!

Group

יְהִי שֵׁם יְיָ מְבֹרָךְ מֵעַתָּה וְעַד עוֹלָם.

Y'hi shem Adonai m'vorach mei-atah v'ad olam.

Praised be the name of God, now and forever.

Leader

יְהִי שֵׁם יְיָ מְבֹרָךְ מֵעַתָּה וְעַד עוֹלָם.
בִּרְשׁוּת הַחֶבְרָה, נְבָרֵךְ אֱלֹהֵינוּ שֶׁאָכַלְנוּ מִשֶּׁלוֹ.

Y'hi shem Adonai m'vorach mei-atah v'ad olam.
Birshut hachevrah, n'vareich Eloheinu she-achalnu mishelo.

Praised be the name of God, now and forever.
Praised be our God, of whose abundance we have eaten.

Group

בָּרוּךְ אֱלֹהֵינוּ שֶׁאָכַלְנוּ מִשֶּׁלוֹ וּבְטוּבוֹ חָיִינוּ.

Baruch Eloheinu she-achalnu mishelo uv'tuvo chayinu.

Praised be our God, of whose abundance we have eaten,
and by whose goodness we live.

Leader

בָּרוּךְ אֱלֹהֵינוּ שֶׁאָכַלְנוּ מִשֶּׁלוֹ וּבְטוּבוֹ חָיֵינוּ.
בָּרוּךְ הוּא וּבָרוּךְ שְׁמוֹ.

Baruch Eloheinu she-achalnu mishelo uv'tuvo chayinu.
Baruch hu uvaruch sh'mo.

Praised be our God, of whose abundance we have eaten,
and by whose goodness we live. Praised be the Eternal God.

בָּרוּךְ אַתָּה יְיָ, אֱלֹהֵינוּ מֶלֶךְ הָעוֹלָם, הַזָּן אֶת־הָעוֹלָם
כֻּלּוֹ בְּטוּבוֹ בְּחֵן בְּחֶסֶד וּבְרַחֲמִים, הוּא נוֹתֵן לֶחֶם
לְכָל־בָּשָׂר כִּי לְעוֹלָם חַסְדּוֹ. וּבְטוּבוֹ הַגָּדוֹל תָּמִיד
לֹא חָסַר לָנוּ, וְאַל יֶחְסַר לָנוּ מָזוֹן לְעוֹלָם וָעֶד.
בַּעֲבוּר שְׁמוֹ הַגָּדוֹל, כִּי הוּא אֵל זָן וּמְפַרְנֵס לַכֹּל
וּמֵטִיב לַכֹּל, וּמֵכִין מָזוֹן לְכָל־בְּרִיּוֹתָיו אֲשֶׁר בָּרָא.
בָּרוּךְ אַתָּה יְיָ, הַזָּן אֶת־הַכֹּל.

Baruch atah Adonai, Eloheinu Melech haolam,
hazan et haolam kulo b'tuvo, b'chein b'chesed uv'rachamim.
Hu notein lechem l'chol basar ki l'olam chasdo.
Uv'tuvo hagadol tamid lo chasar lanu,
v'al yechsar lanu, mazon l'olam va-ed,
baavur sh'mo hagadol.
Ki hu El zan um'farneis lakol umeitiv lakol,
umeichin mazon l'chol b'riyotav asher bara.
Baruch atah Adonai, hazan et hakol.

Sovereign God of the universe, we praise You: Your
goodness sustains the world. You are the God of grace,
love, and compassion, the Source of bread for all who live;
for Your love is everlasting. In Your great goodness we

need never lack for food; You provide food enough for all.
We praise You, O God, Source of food for all who live.

כַּכָּתוּב, וְאָכַלְתָּ וְשָׂבָעְתָּ, וּבֵרַכְתָּ אֶת־יְהֹוָה אֱלֹהֶיךָ
עַל הָאָרֶץ הַטֹּבָה אֲשֶׁר נָתַן לָךְ. בָּרוּךְ אַתָּה יְיָ,
עַל הָאָרֶץ וְעַל הַמָּזוֹן.

Kakatuv, v'achalta v'savata, uveirachta
et Adonai Elohecha al haaretz hatovah asher natan lach.
Baruch atah Adonai, al haaretz v'al hamazon.

As it is written: When you have eaten and are satisfied,
give praise to your God who has given you this good
earth. We praise You, O God, for the earth and for its
sustenance.

וּבְנֵה יְרוּשָׁלַיִם עִיר הַקֹּדֶשׁ בִּמְהֵרָה בְיָמֵינוּ.
בָּרוּךְ אַתָּה יְיָ, בּוֹנֵה בְרַחֲמָיו יְרוּשָׁלָיִם. אָמֵן.

Uv'neih Y'rushalayim ir hakodesh bimheirah v'yameinu.
Baruch atah Adonai, boneh v'rachamav Y'rushalayim. Amen.

Let Jerusalem, the holy city, be renewed in our time.
We praise You, *Adonai*, in compassion You rebuild
Jerusalem. Amen.

הָרַחֲמָן, הוּא יִמְלוֹךְ עָלֵינוּ לְעוֹלָם וָעֶד.
הָרַחֲמָן, הוּא יִתְבָּרַךְ בַּשָּׁמַיִם וּבָאָרֶץ.
הָרַחֲמָן, הוּא יִשְׁלַח בְּרָכָה מְרֻבָּה בַּבַּיִת הַזֶּה,
וְעַל שֻׁלְחָן זֶה שֶׁאָכַלְנוּ עָלָיו.
הָרַחֲמָן, הוּא יִשְׁלַח לָנוּ אֶת אֵלִיָּהוּ הַנָּבִיא, זָכוּר
לַטּוֹב, וִיבַשֶּׂר לָנוּ בְּשׂוֹרוֹת טוֹבוֹת, יְשׁוּעוֹת וְנֶחָמוֹת.

HaRachaman, hu yimloch aleinu l'olam va-ed.
HaRachaman, hu yitbarach bashamayim uvaaretz.
HaRachaman, hu yishlach b'rachah m'rubah babayit hazeh,
v'al shulchan zeh she-achalnu alav.
HaRachaman, hu yishlach lanu et Eliyahu HaNavi,
zachur latov, vivaser lanu b'sorot tovot, y'shuot v'nechamot.

Merciful One, be our God forever. Merciful One, heaven
and earth alike are blessed by Your presence. Merciful
One, bless this house, this table at which we have eaten.
Merciful One, send us tidings of Elijah, glimpses of good
to come, redemption and consolation.

On Shabbat

הָרַחֲמָן, הוּא יַנְחִילֵנוּ יוֹם שֶׁכֻּלּוֹ שַׁבָּת
וּמְנוּחָה לְחַיֵּי הָעוֹלָמִים.

*HaRachaman, hu yanchileinu yom shekulo Shabbat
um'nuchah l'chayei haolamim.*

Merciful One, help us to see the coming of a time when
all is Shabbat.

On Yom Tov

הָרַחֲמָן, הוּא יַנְחִילֵנוּ יוֹם שֶׁכֻּלּוֹ טוֹב.

HaRachaman, hu yanchileinu yom shekulo tov.

Merciful One, help us to see the coming of a time when
all is good.

עֹשֶׂה שָׁלוֹם בִּמְרוֹמָיו, הוּא יַעֲשֶׂה שָׁלוֹם,
עָלֵינוּ וְעַל כָּל־יִשְׂרָאֵל, וְאִמְרוּ: אָמֵן.
יְהֹוָה עֹז לְעַמּוֹ יִתֵּן, יְהֹוָה יְבָרֵךְ אֶת־עַמּוֹ בַשָּׁלוֹם.

Oseh shalom bimromav, hu yaaseh shalom,
aleinu v'al kol Yisrael, v'imru amen.
Adonai oz l'amo yitein, Adonai y'vareich et amo vashalom.

May the Source of peace grant peace to us, to all Israel,
and to all the world. Amen. May the Eternal grant
strength to our people. May the Eternal bless our people
with peace.

On Shabbat (from Psalm 126)

שִׁיר הַמַּעֲלוֹת בְּשׁוּב יְהֹוָה אֶת־שִׁיבַת צִיּוֹן, הָיִינוּ
כְּחֹלְמִים. אָז יִמָּלֵא שְׂחוֹק פִּינוּ, וּלְשׁוֹנֵנוּ רִנָּה. אָז
יֹאמְרוּ בַגּוֹיִם: הִגְדִּיל יְהֹוָה לַעֲשׂוֹת עִם־אֵלֶּה. הִגְדִּיל
יְהֹוָה לַעֲשׂוֹת עִמָּנוּ, הָיִינוּ שְׂמֵחִים. שׁוּבָה יְהֹוָה
אֶת־שְׁבִיתֵנוּ כַּאֲפִיקִים בַּנֶּגֶב. הַזֹּרְעִים בְּדִמְעָה בְּרִנָּה
יִקְצֹרוּ. הָלוֹךְ יֵלֵךְ וּבָכֹה, נֹשֵׂא מֶשֶׁךְ־הַזָּרַע, בֹּא־יָבוֹא
בְרִנָּה נֹשֵׂא אֲלֻמֹּתָיו.

Shir hamaalot,
b'shuv Adonai et shivat Tziyon hayinu k'chol'mim.
Az yimalei s'chok pinu, ul'shoneinu rinah.
Az yom'ru vagoyim: Higdil Adonai laasot im eileh.
Higdil Adonai laasot imanu, hayinu s'meichim.
Shuvah Adonai et sh'viteinu kaafikim baNegev.
Hazor'im b'dimah b'rinah yiktzoru.
Haloch yeileich uvachoh, nosei meshech hazara,
bo yavo v'rinah nosei alumotav.

A pilgrim song. When God restored the exiles to Zion, it
seemed like a dream. Our mouths were filled with laughter,
our tongues with joyful song. Then they said among the
nations: "God has done great things for them." Yes, God
is doing great things for us, and we are joyful. Restore
our fortunes, O God, as streams revive the desert. Then
those who have sown in tears shall reap in joy. Those who
go forth weeping, bearing bags of seeds, shall come home
with shouts of joy, bearing their sheaves.

If there are fewer than three people reciting Birkat HaMazon *together, skip this first section and continue in the middle of page 32.*

Leader

חֲבֵרִים וַחֲבֵרוֹת נְבָרֵךְ!

Chaveirim vachaveirot n'vareich!

Let us praise God!

Group

יְהִי שֵׁם יְיָ מְבֹרָךְ מֵעַתָּה וְעַד עוֹלָם.

Y'hi shem Adonai m'vorach mei-atah v'ad olam.

Praised be the name of God, now and forever.

Leader

יְהִי שֵׁם יְיָ מְבֹרָךְ מֵעַתָּה וְעַד עוֹלָם.
בִּרְשׁוּת הַחֶבְרָה, נְבָרֵךְ אֱלֹהֵינוּ שֶׁאָכַלְנוּ מִשֶּׁלּוֹ.

Y'hi shem Adonai m'vorach mei-atah v'ad olam.
Birshut hachevrah, n'vareich Eloheinu she-achalnu mishelo.

Praised be the name of God, now and forever.
Praised be our God, of whose abundance we have eaten.

Group

בָּרוּךְ אֱלֹהֵינוּ שֶׁאָכַלְנוּ מִשֶּׁלּוֹ וּבְטוּבוֹ חָיִינוּ.

Baruch Eloheinu she-achalnu mishelo uv'tuvo chayinu.

Praised be our God, of whose abundance we have eaten, and by whose goodness we live.

Leader

בָּרוּךְ אֱלֹהֵינוּ שֶׁאָכַלְנוּ מִשֶּׁלוֹ וּבְטוּבוֹ חָיֵינוּ.
בָּרוּךְ הוּא וּבָרוּךְ שְׁמוֹ.

Baruch Eloheinu she-achalnu mishelo uv'tuvo chayinu.
Baruch hu uvaruch sh'mo.

Praised be our God, of whose abundance we have eaten,
and by whose goodness we live. Praised be the Eternal God.

בָּרוּךְ אַתָּה יְיָ, אֱלֹהֵינוּ מֶלֶךְ הָעוֹלָם, הַזָּן אֶת־הָעוֹלָם
כֻּלּוֹ בְּטוּבוֹ, בְּחֵן בְּחֶסֶד וּבְרַחֲמִים. הוּא נוֹתֵן לֶחֶם
לְכָל־בָּשָׂר, כִּי לְעוֹלָם חַסְדּוֹ. וּבְטוּבוֹ הַגָּדוֹל תָּמִיד
לֹא חָסַר לָנוּ, וְאַל יֶחְסַר לָנוּ, מָזוֹן לְעוֹלָם וָעֶד,
בַּעֲבוּר שְׁמוֹ הַגָּדוֹל. כִּי הוּא אֵל זָן וּמְפַרְנֵס לַכֹּל,
וּמֵטִיב לַכֹּל, וּמֵכִין מָזוֹן לְכָל־בְּרִיּוֹתָיו אֲשֶׁר בָּרָא.
בָּרוּךְ אַתָּה יְיָ, הַזָּן אֶת־הַכֹּל.

Baruch atah Adonai, Eloheinu Melech haolam,
hazan et haolam kulo b'tuvo, b'chein b'chesed uv'rachamim.
Hu notein lechem l'chol basar ki l'olam chasdo.
Uv'tuvo hagadol tamid lo chasar lanu,
v'al yechsar lanu, mazon l'olam va-ed,
baavur sh'mo hagadol.
Ki hu El zan um'farneis lakol umeitiv lakol,
umeichin mazon l'chol b'riyotav asher bara.
Baruch atah Adonai, hazan et hakol.

Sovereign God of the universe, we praise You: Your
goodness sustains the world. You are the God of grace,
love, and compassion, the Source of bread for all who live;
for Your love is everlasting. In Your great goodness we

need never lack for food; You provide food enough for all.
We praise You, O God, Source of food for all who live.

נוֹדֶה לְךָ, יְיָ אֱלֹהֵינוּ, עַל שֶׁהִנְחַלְתָּ לַאֲבוֹתֵינוּ
וּלְאִמּוֹתֵינוּ אֶרֶץ חֶמְדָּה טוֹבָה וּרְחָבָה; וְעַל
שֶׁהוֹצֵאתָנוּ, יְיָ אֱלֹהֵינוּ מֵאֶרֶץ מִצְרַיִם; וּפְדִיתָנוּ
מִבֵּית עֲבָדִים; וְעַל בְּרִיתְךָ שֶׁחָתַמְתָּ בִּלְבָבֵנוּ;
וְעַל תּוֹרָתְךָ שֶׁלִּמַּדְתָּנוּ, וְעַל חֻקֶּיךָ שֶׁהוֹדַעְתָּנוּ,
וְעַל חַיִּים חֵן וָחֶסֶד שֶׁחוֹנַנְתָּנוּ, וְעַל אֲכִילַת מָזוֹן
שָׁאַתָּה זָן וּמְפַרְנֵס אוֹתָנוּ תָּמִיד, בְּכָל־יוֹם וּבְכָל־עֵת
וּבְכָל־שָׁעָה.

Nodeh l'cha, Adonai Eloheinu,
al shehinchalta laavoteinu ul'imoteinu
eretz chemdah tovah ur'chavah;
v'al shehotzeitanu, Adonai Eloheinu mei-eretz Mitzrayim;
uf'ditanu mibeit avadim;
v'al b'rit'cha shechatamta bilvaveinu;
v'al Torat'cha shelimadtanu, v'al chukecha shehodatanu,
v'al chayim chein vachesed shechonantanu,
v'al achilat mazon shaatah zan um'farneis otanu tamid,
b'chol yom uv'chol eit uv'chol shaah.

For this good earth that You have entrusted to our
mothers and fathers, and to us; for our deliverance from
bondage; for the covenant You have sealed into our
hearts; for Your life-giving love and grace; for Torah,
our way of life, and for the food that sustains us day by
day, we give You thanks.

וְעַל הַכֹּל, יְיָ אֱלֹהֵינוּ, אֲנַחְנוּ מוֹדִים לָךְ וּמְבָרְכִים אוֹתָךְ. יִתְבָּרַךְ שִׁמְךָ בְּפִי כָל־חַי תָּמִיד לְעוֹלָם וָעֶד, כַּכָּתוּב: וְאָכַלְתָּ וְשָׂבָעְתָּ, וּבֵרַכְתָּ אֶת־יְהֹוָה אֱלֹהֶיךָ עַל הָאָרֶץ הַטֹּבָה אֲשֶׁר נָתַן־לָךְ. בָּרוּךְ אַתָּה יְיָ, עַל־הָאָרֶץ וְעַל־הַמָּזוֹן.

*V'al hakol, Adonai Eloheinu, anachnu modim lach
um'var'chim otach. Yitbarach shimcha
b'fi chol chai tamid l'olam va-ed,
kakatuv: V'achalta v'savata, uveirachta et Adonai Elohecha
al haaretz hatovah asher natan lach.
Baruch atah Adonai, al haaretz v'al hamazon.*

For all this we thank You. Let Your praise ever be on the lips of all who live, as it is written: "When you have eaten and are satisfied, give praise to your God who has given you this good earth." We praise You, O God, for the earth, and for its sustenance.

רַחֵם, יְיָ אֱלֹהֵינוּ, עַל יִשְׂרָאֵל עַמֶּךָ, וְעַל יְרוּשָׁלַיִם עִירֶךָ, וְעַל צִיּוֹן מִשְׁכַּן כְּבוֹדֶךָ. אֱלֹהֵינוּ אָבִינוּ, רְעֵנוּ זוּנֵנוּ, פַּרְנְסֵנוּ וְכַלְכְּלֵנוּ וְהַרְוִיחֵנוּ, וְהַרְוַח־לָנוּ, יְיָ אֱלֹהֵינוּ, מְהֵרָה מִכָּל־צָרוֹתֵינוּ. וְנָא אַל תַּצְרִיכֵנוּ, יְיָ אֱלֹהֵינוּ, לֹא לִידֵי מַתְּנַת בָּשָׂר וָדָם וְלֹא לִידֵי הַלְוָאָתָם, כִּי אִם לְיָדְךָ הַמְּלֵאָה הַפְּתוּחָה הַקְּדוֹשָׁה וְהָרְחָבָה, שֶׁלֹּא נֵבוֹשׁ וְלֹא נִכָּלֵם לְעוֹלָם וָעֶד.

Racheim, Adonai Eloheinu, al Yisrael amecha,
v'al Y'rushalayim irecha, v'al Tziyon mishkan k'vodecha.
Eloheinu Avinu, r'einu zuneinu, parn'seinu v'chalk'leinu
v'harvicheinu, v'harvach lanu, Adonai Eloheinu,
m'heirah mikol tzaroteinu.
V'na al tatzricheinu, Adonai Eloheinu,
lo lidei mat'nat basar vadam v'lo lidei halvaatam,
ki im l'yad'cha ham'lei-ah hap'tuchah hak'doshah v'har'chavah,
shelo neivosh v'lo nikaleim l'olam va-ed.

Eternal God, Source of our being, show compassion for
Israel Your people, Jerusalem Your city, and Zion, the
ancient dwelling-place of Your glory. Guide and sustain
us in all our habitations, and be a help to us in all our
troubles. May we ever be able to help ourselves and one
another, even as we rely on Your open and generous bounty.

On Shabbat

רְצֵה וְהַחֲלִיצֵנוּ, יְיָ אֱלֹהֵינוּ, בְּמִצְוֹתֶיךָ וּבְמִצְוַת יוֹם
הַשְּׁבִיעִי הַשַּׁבָּת הַגָּדוֹל וְהַקָּדוֹשׁ הַזֶּה, כִּי יוֹם זֶה גָּדוֹל
וְקָדוֹשׁ הוּא לְפָנֶיךָ, לִשְׁבָּת־בּוֹ וְלָנוּחַ בּוֹ בְּאַהֲבָה
כְּמִצְוַת רְצוֹנֶךָ. וּבִרְצוֹנְךָ הָנִיחַ לָנוּ, יְיָ אֱלֹהֵינוּ, שֶׁלֹא
תְהֵא צָרָה וְיָגוֹן וַאֲנָחָה בְּיוֹם מְנוּחָתֵנוּ. וְהַרְאֵנוּ, יְיָ
אֱלֹהֵינוּ, בְּנֶחָמַת צִיּוֹן עִירֶךָ וּבְבִנְיַן יְרוּשָׁלַיִם עִיר
קָדְשֶׁךָ, כִּי אַתָּה הוּא בַּעַל הַיְשׁוּעוֹת וּבַעַל הַנֶּחָמוֹת.

R'tzeih v'hachalitzeinu, Adonai Eloheinu, b'mitzvotecha
uv'mitzvat yom hash'vi-i
haShabbat hagadol v'hakadosh hazeh,
ki yom zeh gadol v'kadosh hu l'fanecha,
lishbot bo v'lanuach bo b'ahavah k'mitzvat r'tzonecha.

Uvir'tzon'cha haniach lanu, Adonai Eloheinu,
shelo t'hei tzarah v'yagon vaanachah b'yom m'nuchateinu.
V'hareinu, Adonai Eloheinu, b'nechamat Tziyon irecha
uv'vinyan Y'rushalayim ir kodshecha,
ki atah hu baal hay'shuot uvaal hanechamot.

Eternal God, strengthen our resolve to live by Your mitzvot,
and especially the mitzvah of the seventh day, the great
and holy Sabbath, the day of rest and serenity, of loving
reflection upon Your will. Source of deliverance and of
consolation, give us this day rest from sorrow, anguish,
and pain, and renew our vision of a more beautiful world.

וּבְנֵה יְרוּשָׁלַיִם עִיר הַקֹּדֶשׁ בִּמְהֵרָה בְיָמֵינוּ.
בָּרוּךְ אַתָּה יְיָ, בּוֹנֶה בְרַחֲמָיו יְרוּשָׁלָיִם. אָמֵן.

Uv'neih Y'rushalayim ir hakodesh bimheirah v'yameinu.
Baruch atah Adonai, boneh v'rachamav Y'rushalayim. Amen.

Let Jerusalem, the holy city, be renewed in our time.
We praise You, *Adonai*; in compassion You rebuild
Jerusalem. Amen.

בָּרוּךְ אַתָּה יְיָ אֱלֹהֵינוּ מֶלֶךְ הָעוֹלָם, הָאֵל אָבִינוּ
מַלְכֵּנוּ, אַדִּירֵנוּ, בּוֹרְאֵנוּ, גּוֹאֲלֵנוּ, יוֹצְרֵנוּ, קְדוֹשֵׁנוּ,
קְדוֹשׁ יַעֲקֹב, רוֹעֵנוּ רוֹעֵה יִשְׂרָאֵל, הַמֶּלֶךְ הַטּוֹב
וְהַמֵּטִיב לַכֹּל, שֶׁבְּכָל־יוֹם וָיוֹם הוּא הֵטִיב, הוּא
מֵטִיב, הוּא יֵיטִיב לָנוּ. הוּא גְמָלָנוּ, הוּא גוֹמְלֵנוּ הוּא
יִגְמְלֵנוּ לָעַד, לְחֵן וּלְחֶסֶד וּלְרַחֲמִים וּלְרֶוַח, הַצָּלָה

וְהַצְלָחָה, בְּרָכָה וִישׁוּעָה, נֶחָמָה, פַּרְנָסָה וְכַלְכָּלָה, וְרַחֲמִים וְחַיִּים וְשָׁלוֹם, וְכָל־טוֹב, וּמִכָּל־טוֹב לְעוֹלָם אַל יְחַסְּרֵנוּ.

Baruch atah Adonai, Eloheinu Melech haolam,
ha-El Avinu Malkeinu Adireinu,
Bor'einu, Goaleinu, Yotz'reinu, K'dosheinu, K'dosh Yaakov,
Ro-einu Ro-eih Yisrael, HaMelech hatov v'hameitiv lakol,
sheb'chol yom vayom hu heitiv, hu meitiv, hu yeitiv lanu.
Hu g'malanu, hu gom'leinu, hu yigm'leinu laad,
l'chein ul'chesed ul'rachamim ul'revach, hatzalah v'hatzlachah,
b'rachah vishuah, nechamah, parnasah v'chalkalah,
v'rachamim v'chayim v'shalom, v'chol tov,
umikol tov l'olam al y'chas'reinu.

We praise You, divine Parent of Israel, Source of
liberating power and vision, of all that is holy and good.
You have shown us love and kindness always; day by day
You grant us grace and compassion, deliverance and
freedom, prosperity and blessing, life and peace.

הָרַחֲמָן, הוּא יִמְלוֹךְ עָלֵינוּ לְעוֹלָם וָעֶד.
הָרַחֲמָן, הוּא יִתְבָּרַךְ בַּשָּׁמַיִם וּבָאָרֶץ.
הָרַחֲמָן, הוּא יִשְׁתַּבַּח לְדוֹר דּוֹרִים, וְיִתְפָּאַר בָּנוּ לָעַד
וּלְנֵצַח נְצָחִים, וְיִתְהַדַּר בָּנוּ לָעַד וּלְעוֹלְמֵי עוֹלָמִים.
הָרַחֲמָן, הוּא יְבָרֵךְ אֶת מְדִינַת יִשְׂרָאֵל וְאֶת אַחֵינוּ
וְאַחְיוֹתֵינוּ בְּרַחֲבֵי הָעוֹלָם.
הָרַחֲמָן, הוּא יְפַרְנְסֵנוּ בְּכָבוֹד.
הָרַחֲמָן, הוּא יִשְׁבּוֹר עֻלֵּנוּ מֵעַל צַוָּארֵנוּ.

הָרַחֲמָן, הוּא יִשְׁלַח בְּרָכָה מְרֻבָּה בַּבַּיִת הַזֶּה וְעַל שֻׁלְחָן זֶה שֶׁאָכַלְנוּ עָלָיו.

הָרַחֲמָן, הוּא יִשְׁלַח לָנוּ אֶת אֵלִיָּהוּ הַנָּבִיא, זָכוּר לַטּוֹב, וִיבַשֶּׂר לָנוּ בְּשׂוֹרוֹת טוֹבוֹת, יְשׁוּעוֹת וְנֶחָמוֹת.

הָרַחֲמָן, הוּא יְזַכֵּנוּ לִימוֹת הַגְּאֻלָּה וּלְחַיֵּי הָעוֹלָם הַבָּא.

HaRachaman, hu yimloch aleinu l'olam va-ed.
HaRachaman, hu yitbarach bashamayim uvaaretz.
HaRachaman, hu yishtabach l'dor dorim,
v'yitpaar banu laad ul'neitzach n'tzachim,
v'yit-hadar banu laad ul'ol'mei olamim.
HaRachaman, hu y'vareich et m'dinat Yisrael
v'et acheinu v'achayoteinu b'rochvei haolam.
HaRachaman, hu y'farn'seinu b'chavod.
HaRachaman, hu yishbor uleinu mei-al tzavareinu,
v'hu yolicheinu kom'miyut l'artzeinu.
HaRachaman, hu yishlach b'rachah m'rubah babayit hazeh
v'al shulchan zeh she-achalnu alav.
HaRachaman, hu yishlach lanu et Eliyahu HaNavi,
zachur latov, vivaser lanu b'sorot tovot, y'shuot v'nechamot.
HaRachaman, hu y'zakeinu limot hag'ulah
ul'chayei haolam haba.

Merciful One, be our God forever. Merciful One, heaven and earth alike are blessed by Your presence. Merciful One, let all the generations proclaim Your glory. Merciful One, bless the State of Israel and our brothers and sisters throughout the world. Merciful One, help us to sustain ourselves in honor. Merciful One, break the yoke of oppression from off our necks. Merciful One, bless this house, this table at which we have eaten.

Merciful One, send us tidings of Elijah, glimpses of good to come, of redemption and consolation. Merciful One, find us worthy of witnessing a time of redemption and of attaining eternal life.

הָרַחֲמָן, הוּא יְבָרֵךְ אוֹתָנוּ וְאֶת־כָּל־אֲשֶׁר לָנוּ, כְּמוֹ שֶׁנִּתְבָּרְכוּ אֲבוֹתֵינוּ אַבְרָהָם, יִצְחָק, וְיַעֲקֹב, וְאִמּוֹתֵינוּ שָׂרָה, רִבְקָה, רָחֵל וְלֵאָה, בַּכֹּל מִכֹּל כֹּל, כֵּן יְבָרֵךְ אוֹתָנוּ כֻּלָּנוּ יַחַד, בִּבְרָכָה שְׁלֵמָה, וְנֹאמַר: אָמֵן.

HaRachaman, hu y'vareich otanu v'et kol asher lanu,
k'mo shenitbar'chu avoteinu Avraham, Yitzchak, v'Yaakov,
v'imoteinu Sarah, Rivkah, Racheil v'Lei-ah, bakol mikol kol,
kein y'vareich otanu kulanu yachad,
bivrachah sh'leimah, v'nomar: Amen.

Merciful One, bless us and all our dear ones; as You blessed our ancestors Abraham, Isaac, and Jacob; Sarah, Rebekah, Leah, and Rachel, so bless us, one and all; and let us say: Amen.

בַּמָּרוֹם יְלַמְּדוּ עָלֵינוּ זְכוּת שֶׁתְּהֵא לְמִשְׁמֶרֶת שָׁלוֹם; וְנִשָּׂא בְרָכָה מֵאֵת יְיָ וּצְדָקָה מֵאֱלֹהֵי יִשְׁעֵנוּ, וְנִמְצָא חֵן וְשֵׂכֶל טוֹב בְּעֵינֵי אֱלֹהִים וְאָדָם.

Bamarom y'lam'du aleinu z'chut shet'hei l'mishmeret shalom;
v'nisa v'rachah mei-eit Adonai utz'dakah meiElohei yisheinu,
v'nimtza chein v'seichel tov b'einei Elohim v'adam.

May we receive blessings from the Eternal One, kindness from God our help, and may we all find divine and human grace and favor.

On Shabbat

הָרַחֲמָן, הוּא יַנְחִילֵנוּ יוֹם שֶׁכֻּלּוֹ שַׁבָּת
וּמְנוּחָה לְחַיֵּי הָעוֹלָמִים.

*HaRachaman, hu yanchileinu yom shekulo Shabbat
um'nuchah l'chayei haolamim.*

Merciful One, help us to see the coming of a time that
is all Shabbat.

On Yom Tov

הָרַחֲמָן, הוּא יַנְחִילֵנוּ יוֹם שֶׁכֻּלּוֹ טוֹב.

HaRachaman, hu yanchileinu yom shekulo tov.

Merciful One, help us to see the coming of a time when
all is good.

עֹשֶׂה שָׁלוֹם בִּמְרוֹמָיו, הוּא יַעֲשֶׂה שָׁלוֹם,
עָלֵינוּ וְעַל כָּל־יִשְׂרָאֵל, וְאִמְרוּ: אָמֵן.

*Oseh shalom bimromav, hu yaaseh shalom,
aleinu v'al kol Yisrael, v'imru: Amen.*

May the Source of perfect peace grant peace to us,
to all Israel, and to all the world. Amen.

הוֹדוּ לַיהוָה כִּי־טוֹב, כִּי לְעוֹלָם חַסְדּוֹ.
פּוֹתֵחַ אֶת־יָדֶךָ, וּמַשְׂבִּיעַ לְכָל־חַי רָצוֹן.
בָּרוּךְ הַגֶּבֶר אֲשֶׁר יִבְטַח בַּיהוָה, וְהָיָה יְהוָה מִבְטַחוֹ.

Hodu l'Adonai ki tov, ki l'olam chasdo.
Potei-ach et yadecha, umasbia l'chol chai ratzon.
Baruch hagever asher yivtach b'Adonai,
v'hayah Adonai mivtacho.

Give thanks to God, who is good, whose love is
everlasting, whose hand is open to feed all that lives.
Blessed are you who trust in God, who make God
your stronghold.

יְהֹוָה עֹז לְעַמּוֹ יִתֵּן, יְהֹוָה יְבָרֵךְ אֶת־עַמּוֹ בַשָּׁלוֹם.

Adonai oz l'amo yitein, Adonai y'vareich et amo vashalom.

Eternal God: give strength to Your people; Eternal God:
bless Your people with peace.

SHEVA B'RACHOT: THE SEVEN WEDDING BLESSINGS

בָּרוּךְ אַתָּה יְיָ, אֱלֹהֵינוּ מֶלֶךְ הָעוֹלָם, בּוֹרֵא פְּרִי הַגָּפֶן.

Baruch atah Adonai, Eloheinu Melech haolam,
borei p'ri hagafen.

We praise You, Eternal God, Sovereign of the universe,
Creator of the fruit of the vine.

בָּרוּךְ אַתָּה יְיָ, אֱלֹהֵינוּ מֶלֶךְ הָעוֹלָם,
שֶׁהַכֹּל בָּרָא לִכְבוֹדוֹ.

Baruch atah Adonai, Eloheinu Melech haolam,
shehakol bara lichvodo.

Praised be the One whose glory we find in all that
we behold.

בָּרוּךְ אַתָּה יְיָ, אֱלֹהֵינוּ מֶלֶךְ הָעוֹלָם, יוֹצֵר הָאָדָם.

Baruch atah Adonai, Eloheinu Melech haolam,
yotzeir haadam.

Praised be the Creator of humankind.

בָּרוּךְ אַתָּה יְיָ, אֱלֹהֵינוּ מֶלֶךְ הָעוֹלָם, אֲשֶׁר יָצַר
אֶת־הָאָדָם בְּצַלְמוֹ, בְּצֶלֶם דְּמוּת תַּבְנִיתוֹ, וְהִתְקִין לוֹ
מִמֶּנּוּ בִּנְיַן עֲדֵי־עַד. בָּרוּךְ אַתָּה יְיָ, יוֹצֵר הָאָדָם.

Baruch atah Adonai, Eloheinu Melech haolam,
asher yatzar et haadam b'tzalmo, b'tzelem d'mut tavnito,
v'hitkin lo mimenu banyan adei ad.
Baruch atah Adonai, yotzeir haadam.

Praised be our God, Creator of woman and man,
a single human fabric woven of love. You have made
us in Your own image, Your own likeness, and we give
thanks and praise.

שׂוֹשׂ תָּשִׂישׂ וְתָגֵל הָעֲקָרָה, בְּקִבּוּץ בָּנֶיהָ לְתוֹכָהּ
בְּשִׂמְחָה. בָּרוּךְ אַתָּה יְיָ, מְשַׂמֵּחַ צִיּוֹן בְּבָנֶיהָ.

Sos tasis v'tageil haakarah,
b'kibutz baneha l'tochah b'simchah.
Baruch atah Adonai, m'samei-ach Tziyon b'vaneha.

You have filled Zion's mouth with song: her children
have come back to her in joy! We give thanks to the
One who gladdens Zion through her children.

שַׂמֵּחַ תְּשַׂמַּח רֵעִים הָאֲהוּבִים, כְּשַׂמֵּחֲךָ יְצִירְךָ בְּגַן
עֵדֶן מִקֶּדֶם. בָּרוּךְ אַתָּה יְיָ, מְשַׂמֵּחַ חָתָן וְכַלָּה.

Samei-ach t'samach rei-im haahuvim,
k'sameichacha y'tzir'cha b'Gan Eiden mikedem.
Baruch atah Adonai, m'samei-ach chatan v'chalah.

To these Your children, by love made one, all delight
and gladness give. Renew their lives, refresh their hearts,
show them both the joy of Eden. Eternal God, we
praise You, for You cause man and woman to rejoice
in marriage.

בָּרוּךְ אַתָּה יְיָ, אֱלֹהֵינוּ מֶלֶךְ הָעוֹלָם, אֲשֶׁר בָּרָא
שָׂשׂוֹן וְשִׂמְחָה, חָתָן וְכַלָּה, גִּילָה רִנָּה דִּיצָה
וְחֶדְוָה, אַהֲבָה וְאַחֲוָה, שָׁלוֹם וְרֵעוּת. מְהֵרָה, יְיָ
אֱלֹהֵינוּ, יִשָּׁמַע בְּעָרֵי יְהוּדָה וּבְחוּצוֹת יְרוּשָׁלָיִם,
קוֹל שָׂשׂוֹן וְקוֹל שִׂמְחָה, קוֹל חָתָן וְקוֹל כַּלָּה, קוֹל
מִצְהֲלוֹת חֲתָנִים מֵחֻפָּתָם, וּנְעָרִים מִמִּשְׁתֵּה נְגִינָתָם.
בָּרוּךְ אַתָּה יְיָ, מְשַׂמֵּחַ חָתָן עִם הַכַּלָּה.

Baruch atah Adonai, Eloheinu Melech haolam,
asher bara sason v'simchah chatan v'chalah,
gilah rinah ditzah v'chedvah,
ahavah v'achavah, shalom v'rei-ut.
M'heirah, Adonai Eloheinu, yishama
b'arei Y'hudah uv'chutzot Y'rushalayim,
kol sason v'kol simchah, kol chatan v'kol kalah,
kol mitzhalot chatanim meichupatam,
un'arim mimishteih n'ginatam.
Baruch atah Adonai, m'samei-ach chatan im hakalah.

We give thanks for joy and gladness, happiness and exaltation, love and harmony, peace and friendship. Speedily let there be heard in the streets of Jerusalem and the cities of Judah, in earth's four corners, the cry of joy and the shout of gladness, the tender song of woman and man, the happy sounds of the wedding feast. Praised be the One who causes woman and man to rejoice in marriage.

יְבָרֶכְךָ יְהֹוָה וְיִשְׁמְרֶךָ. יָאֵר יְהֹוָה פָּנָיו אֵלֶיךָ וִיחֻנֶּךָּ. יִשָּׂא יְהֹוָה פָּנָיו אֵלֶיךָ וְיָשֵׂם לְךָ שָׁלוֹם.

Y'varech'cha Adonai v'yishm'recha.
Ya-eir Adonai panav eilecha vichuneka.
Yisa Adonai panav eilecha v'yaseim l'cha shalom.

May God bless and keep you. May God look kindly upon you, and be gracious to you. May God reach out to You in tenderness and give you peace.

THANKSGIVING FOR OTHER FOODS

When no bread has been eaten, recite this blessing.

בָּרוּךְ אַתָּה יְיָ, אֱלֹהֵינוּ מֶלֶךְ הָעוֹלָם, בּוֹרֵא נְפָשׁוֹת רַבּוֹת וְחֶסְרוֹנָן עַל כָּל־מַה שֶׁבָּרֵאתָ לְהַחֲיוֹת בָּהֶם נֶפֶשׁ כָּל־חָי. בָּרוּךְ חֵי הָעוֹלָמִים.

Baruch atah Adonai, Eloheinu Melech haolam,
borei n'fashot rabot v'chesronan al kol mah shebarata
l'hachayot bahem nefesh kol chai.
Baruch chei haolamim.

We praise You, Eternal God, Sovereign of the universe, Creator of the living and their needs. Life of all life, we thank You for the food that keeps us alive.

Sources for songs can be found on pages 74–75. All songs can be found in The Complete Shireinu, *published by Transcontinental Music Publications/URJ Press and available at* **www.transcontinentalmusic.com**.

BO-I KALAH

בּוֹאִי כַלָּה! לְכָה דוֹדִי לִקְרַאת כַּלָּה,
פְּנֵי שַׁבָּת נְקַבְּלָה.

Bo-i kalah! L'chah dodi likrat kalah,
p'nei Shabbat n'kab'lah.

Enter, O bride! Come, my beloved, to greet the bride;
let us welcome the Shabbat presence.

DODI LI

דּוֹדִי לִי וַאֲנִי לוֹ הָרֹעֶה בַּשּׁוֹשַׁנִּים.
מִי זֹאת עֹלָה מִן־הַמִּדְבָּר?
מְקֻטֶּרֶת מוֹר וּלְבוֹנָה. אֲנִי לְדוֹדִי וְדוֹדִי לִי.
לִבַּבְתִּנִי אֲחֹתִי כַלָּה. עוּרִי צָפוֹן וּבוֹאִי תֵימָן.

Dodi li vaani lo haro-eh bashoshanim.
Mi zot olah min hamidbar? M'kuteret mor ul'vonah.
Ani l'dodi v'dodi li. Libavtini achoti chalah.
Uri tzafon uvo-i teiman.

My beloved is mine and I am my beloved's. Who feeds among the lilies? Who is this coming up from the desert, burning myrrh and frankincense? I am my beloved's and my beloved is mine. You have ravished my heart, my sister, my bride. Awake, O north wind. Come, O south wind.

D'ROR YIKRA

דְּרוֹר יִקְרָא לְבֵן עִם בַּת וְיִנְצָרְכֶם כְּמוֹ בָבַת,
נְעִים שִׁמְכֶם וְלֹא יֻשְׁבַּת, שְׁבוּ וְנוּחוּ בְּיוֹם שַׁבָּת.

דְּרֹשׁ נָוִי וְאוּלָמִי וְאוֹת יֶשַׁע עֲשֵׂה עִמִּי,
נְטַע שׂוֹרֵק בְּתוֹךְ כַּרְמִי, שְׁעֵה שַׁוְעַת בְּנֵי עַמִּי.

D'ror yikra l'ven im bat v'yintzorchem k'mo vavat,
n'im shimchem v'lo yushbat, sh'vu v'nuchu b'yom Shabbat.

D'rosh navi v'ulami, v'ot yesha aseih imi,
n'ta soreik b'toch karmi, sh'eih shavat b'nei ami.

May God proclaim freedom for all sons and daughters and keep you as the apple of God's eye. Pleasant is your name; it will not be destroyed. Repose, relax on Shabbat.

Revisit My holy Temple, and give Me a sign of deliverance. Plant a vine in My vineyard. Look to My people; hear their laments.

EILEH CHAM'DAH LIBI

אֵלֶּה חָמְדָה לִבִּי חוּסָה נָא וְאַל נָא תִּתְעַלֵּם.

Eileh cham'dah libi chusah na v'al na titaleim.

My heart took pleasure in these. Have pity and do not vanish.

EIT DODIM

עֵת דּוֹדִים כַּלָּה בּוֹאִי לְגַנִּי.
פָּרְחָה הַגֶּפֶן הֵנֵצוּ הָרִמּוֹנִים.

Eit dodim kalah bo-i l'gani.
Par'chah hagefen heineitzu harimonim.

It is a time for lovers. Come into my garden, my bride.
The vines are blossoming. The pomegranates are budding.

HARACHAMAN

הָרַחֲמָן, הוּא יַנְחִילֵנוּ יוֹם שֶׁכֻּלּוֹ שַׁבָּת וּמְנוּחָה.

HaRachaman, hu yanchileinu yom shekulo
Shabbat um'nuchah.

All Merciful, may we inherit Shabbat and rest.

KI ESHM'RAH SHABBAT

כִּי אֶשְׁמְרָה שַׁבָּת אֵל יִשְׁמְרֵנִי.
אוֹת הִיא לְעוֹלְמֵי עַד בֵּינוֹ וּבֵינִי.

Ki eshm'rah Shabbat El yishm'reini.
Ot hi l'olmei ad beino uveini.

As I observe Shabbat, God watches over me.
It is a sign forever between God and me.

L'CHU N'RAN'NAH

לְכוּ נְרַנְּנָה לַיְיָ. נָרִיעָה לְצוּר יִשְׁעֵנוּ.

L'chu n'ran'nah l'Adonai, nariah l'tzur yisheinu.

Go forth singing songs of joy to the Eternal.
Let us shout to our Savior.

MAH YAFEH HAYOM

מַה יָּפֶה הַיּוֹם, שַׁבָּת שָׁלוֹם.

Mah yafeh hayom, Shabbat shalom!

How lovely today is. May you have a peaceful Shabbat.

MIZMOR SHIR

מִזְמוֹר שִׁיר לְיוֹם הַשַּׁבָּת. טוֹב לְהֹדוֹת לַיְיָ
וּלְזַמֵּר לְשִׁמְךָ עֶלְיוֹן.
לְהַגִּיד בַּבֹּקֶר חַסְדֶּךָ, וֶאֱמוּנָתְךָ בַּלֵּילוֹת
עֲלֵי־עָשׂוֹר וַעֲלֵי־נָבֶל, עֲלֵי הִגָּיוֹן בְּכִנּוֹר.

Mizmor shir l'yom haShabbat.
Tov l'hodot l'Adonai, ul'zameir l'shimcha Elyon.

L'hagid baboker chasdecha, ve-emunat'cha baleilot.
Alei asor vaalei navel, alei higayon b'chinor.

A psalm, a song for the Shabbat. It is good to give thanks
to *Adonai*, to sing hymns to Your name, O Most High!

To tell of Your loving-kindness in the morning and
Your faithfulness at night; to pluck the strings, to sound
the lute; to make the harp vibrate.

OD YISHAMA

עוֹד יִשָּׁמַע בְּעָרֵי יְהוּדָה וּבְחֻצוֹת יְרוּשָׁלַיִם
קוֹל שָׂשׂוֹן וְקוֹל שִׂמְחָה, קוֹל חָתָן וְקוֹל כַּלָּה.

*Od yishama b'arei Y'hudah uv'chutzot Y'rushalayim
kol sason v'kol simchah, kol chatan v'kol kalah.*

There shall yet be heard in the cities of Judah and the
outskirts of Jerusalem the sounds of gladness and joy,
the voice of bridegroom and bride.

ROM'MU

רוֹמְמוּ יְיָ אֱלֹהֵינוּ, וְהִשְׁתַּחֲווּ לְהַר קָדְשׁוֹ.
כִּי קָדוֹשׁ יְיָ אֱלֹהֵינוּ.

*Rom'mu Adonai Eloheinu, v'hishtachavu l'har kodsho,
ki kadosh Adonai Eloheinu.*

Let us exalt *Adonai* our God and worship at God's holy
mountain. For *Adonai* our God is holy.

SHIR HAMAALOT

שִׁיר הַמַּעֲלוֹת, בְּשׁוּב יְהֹוָה אֶת־שִׁיבַת צִיּוֹן, הָיִינוּ
כְּחֹלְמִים. אָז יִמָּלֵא שְׂחוֹק פִּינוּ, וּלְשׁוֹנֵנוּ רִנָּה. אָז
יֹאמְרוּ בַגּוֹיִם: הִגְדִּיל יְהֹוָה לַעֲשׂוֹת עִם־אֵלֶּה. הִגְדִּיל
יְהֹוָה לַעֲשׂוֹת עִמָּנוּ, הָיִינוּ שְׂמֵחִים.

*Shir hamaalot,
b'shuv Adonai et shivat Tziyon hayinu k'chol'mim.
Az yimalei s'chok pinu, ul'shoneinu rinah.
Az yom'ru vagoyim, higdil Adonai laasot im eileh.
Higdil Adonai laasot imanu, hayinu s'meichim.*

A song of ascents: When *Adonai* brought the exiles back to Zion it was like a dream. Then our mouths were filled with laughter and our tongues with song. Then was it said among the nations: "*Adonai* has done great things for them." Truly, *Adonai* has done great things for us.

TZADIK KATAMAR

צַדִּיק כַּתָּמָר יִפְרָח, כְּאֶרֶז בַּלְּבָנוֹן יִשְׂגֶּה.
שְׁתוּלִים בְּבֵית יְיָ, בְּחַצְרוֹת אֱלֹהֵינוּ יַפְרִיחוּ.
עוֹד יְנוּבוּן בְּשֵׂיבָה, דְּשֵׁנִים וְרַעֲנַנִּים יִהְיוּ,
לְהַגִּיד כִּי יָשָׁר יְיָ, צוּרִי, וְלֹא עַוְלָתָה בּוֹ.

Tzadik katamar yifrach, k'erez bal'vanon yisgeh.
Sh'tulim b'veit Adonai, b'chatzrot Eloheinu yafrichu.

Od y'nuvun b'seivah, d'sheinim v'raananim yihyu
l'hagid ki yashar Adonai, tzuri, v'lo avlatah bo.

A righteous person will flourish like a date palm. Like a cedar in Lebanon they will grow tall. Planted in the house of the Eternal, in the courtyards of our God they will flourish.

They will still be fruitful in old age, vigorous and fresh they will be to declare that the Eternal is just, my Rock, in whom there is no wrong.

V'TAHEIR LIBEINU

וְטַהֵר לִבֵּנוּ לְעָבְדְּךָ בֶּאֱמֶת.

V'taheir libeinu l'ovd'cha be-emet.

Purify our hearts to serve You in truth.

Y'DID NEFESH

יְדִיד נֶפֶשׁ, אָב הָרַחֲמָן, מְשׁוֹךְ עַבְדְּךָ אֶל רְצוֹנֶךְ:
יָרוּץ עַבְדְּךָ כְּמוֹ אַיָּל יִשְׁתַּחֲוֶה אֶל מוּל הֲדָרֶךְ.

Y'did nefesh, av harachaman, m'shoch avd'cha el r'tzonecha:
yarutz avd'cha k'mo ayal yishtachaveh el mul hadarecha.

Beloved of the soul, Source of mercy, draw Your
servant into Your arms; I leap like a deer to stand in
awe before You.

YOM ZEH L'YISRAEL

יוֹם זֶה לְיִשְׂרָאֵל אוֹרָה וְשִׂמְחָה, שַׁבָּת מְנוּחָה.

Yom zeh l'Yisrael orah v'simchah, Shabbat m'nuchah.

This is Israel's day of light and joy, a Shabbat of rest.

⬛ *Z'MIROT L'CHOL YOM:* SONGS FOR EVERY DAY

Sources for songs can be found on pages 75–77. All songs can be found in The Complete Shireinu, *published by Transcontinental Music Publications/URJ Press and available at* **www.transcontinentalmusic.com**.

ADONAI OZ

יְהֹוָה עֹז לְעַמּוֹ יִתֵּן,
יְהֹוָה יְבָרֵךְ אֶת־עַמּוֹ בַשָּׁלוֹם.

Adonai oz l'amo yitein,
Adonai y'vareich et amo vashalom.

May God give strength to God's people.
May God bless God's people with peace.

AM YISRAEL CHAI

עַם יִשְׂרָאֵל חַי! עוֹד אָבִינוּ חַי!

Am Yisrael chai! Od Avinu chai!

The people of Israel lives! Our God yet lives!

ANI V'ATAH

אֲנִי וְאַתָּה נְשַׁנֶּה אֶת הָעוֹלָם,
אֲנִי וְאַתָּה, אָז יָבוֹאוּ כְּבָר כֻּלָּם.

אָמְרוּ אֶת זֶה קֹדֶם לְפָנַי, (זֶה) לֹא מְשַׁנֶּה.
אֲנִי וְאַתָּה נְשַׁנֶּה אֶת הָעוֹלָם.

אֲנִי וְאַתָּה נְנַסֶּה מֵהַתְחָלָה;
יִהְיֶה לָנוּ רַע, אֵין דָּבָר, זֶה לֹא נוֹרָא.

Ani v'atah n'shaneh et haolam,
ani v'atah, az yavo-u k'var kulam.

Am'ru et zeh kodem l'fanai, (zeh) lo m'shaneh.
Ani v'atah n'shaneh et haolam.

Ani v'atah n'naseh meihat-chalah;
yihyeh lanu ra, ein davar, zeh lo nora.

You and I will change the world, you and I, then all
will join us.

Though it's been said before, it doesn't matter. You and
I will change the world.

You and I will start from the beginning. It may be
difficult, but it's nothing, it's not so terrible.

ASHREI

אַשְׁרֵי יוֹשְׁבֵי בֵיתֶךָ, עוֹד יְהַלְלוּךָ סֶּלָה.
אַשְׁרֵי הָעָם שֶׁכָּכָה לּוֹ, אַשְׁרֵי הָעָם שֶׁיְיָ אֱלֹהָיו.

Ashrei yosh'vei veitecha, od y'hal'lucha selah.
Ashrei haam shekachah lo, ashrei haam she-Adonai Elohav.

Happy are those who dwell in Your house; they are
always praising You. Happy the people that is so situated;
happy the people whose God is the Eternal.

BASHANAH HABAAH

בַּשָּׁנָה הַבָּאָה נֵשֵׁב עַל הַמִּרְפֶּסֶת
וְנִסְפֹּר צִפֳּרִים נוֹדְדוֹת
יְלָדִים בְּחֻפְשָׁה יְשַׂחֲקוּ תּוֹפֶסֶת
בֵּין הַבַּיִת לְבֵין הַשָּׂדוֹת.

עוֹד תִּרְאֶה, עוֹד תִּרְאֶה כַּמָּה טוֹב יִהְיֶה
בַּשָּׁנָה בַּשָּׁנָה הַבָּאָה.

עֲנָבִים אֲדֻמִּים יַבְשִׁילוּ עַד הָעֶרֶב
וְיֻגְּשׁוּ צוֹנְנִים לַשֻּׁלְחָן
וְרוּחוֹת רְדוּמִים יִשְׂאוּ עַל אֵם הַדֶּרֶךְ
עִתּוֹנִים יְשָׁנִים כְּעָנָן.

בַּשָּׁנָה הַבָּאָה נִפְרֹשׂ כַּפּוֹת יָדַיִם
מוּל הָאוֹר הַנִּגָּר הַלָּבָן
אֲנָפָה לְבָנָה תִּפְרֹשׂ בָּאוֹר כְּנָפַיִם
וְהַשֶּׁמֶשׁ תִּזְרַח בְּתוֹכָן.

Bashanah habaah neisheiv al hamirpeset
v'nispor tziporim nod'dot.
Y'ladim b'chufshah y'sachaku tofeset
bein habayit l'vein hasadot.

Od tireh, od tireh kamah tov yihyeh
bashanah bashanah habaah.

Anavim adumim yavshilu ad ha-erev
v'yug'shu tzon'nim lashulchan.
V'ruchot r'dumim yisu al eim haderech
itonim y'shanim k'anan.

Bashanah habaah nifros kapot yadayim
mul haor hanigar halavan.
Anafah l'vanah tifros baor k'nafayim
v'hashemesh tizrach b'tochan.

Next year we will sit on the porch and count migrating birds. Children on vacation will play catch between the house and the fields.

You will yet see how good it will be next year.

Red grapes will ripen till the evening and will be served chilled to the table. And languid winds will carry to the crossroads old newspapers as a cloud.

Next year we will spread our own hands toward the radiant light. A white heron like a light will spread her wings and within them the sun will rise.

BAYOM HAHU

בַּיּוֹם הַהוּא יִהְיֶה יְיָ אֶחָד וּשְׁמוֹ אֶחָד.

Bayom hahu yihyeh Adonai echad ush'mo echad.

On that day, God shall be One and God's name shall be One.

B'MAKOM

בְּמָקוֹם שֶׁאֵין אֲנָשִׁים הִשְׁתַּדֵּל לִהְיוֹת אִישׁ.

B'makom she-ein anashim hishtadeil lihyot ish.

In a place where there are no human beings, you must strive to be human.

B'TZELEM ELOHIM

Yeah, yeah, yeah, yeah, yeah.

We all got a life to live, we all got a gift to give.
Just open your heart and let it out.
We all got a peace to bring, we all got a song to sing.
Just open your heart and let it out. Yeah!

When I reach out to you and you to me,
We become *b'tzelem Elohim.*
When we share our hopes and our dreams,
Each one of us, *b'tzelem Elohim.*

We all got a tale to tell, we all want to speak it well.
Just open your heart and let it out.
We all got a mountain to climb, we all got a truth
     to find.
Just open your heart and let it out. Yeah!

CHORUS

Part A	Part B
B'reishit bara Elohim.	*B'reishit bara Elohim,* all our hopes, all our dreams.
(repeat)	*B'reishit bara Elohim,* each one of us, *b'tzelem Elohim.*
	(repeat)

EITZ CHAYIM HI

עֵץ חַיִּים הִיא לַמַּחֲזִיקִים בָּהּ וְתֹמְכֶיהָ מְאֻשָּׁר.

Eitz chayim hi lamachazikim bah v'tom'cheha m'ushar.

It is a tree of life to those who hold it fast and all who support it find happiness.

GESHER TZAR M'OD

כָּל הָעוֹלָם כֻּלּוֹ גֶּשֶׁר צַר מְאֹד
וְהָעִקָּר לֹא לְפַחֵד כְּלָל.

Kol haolam kulo gesher tzar m'od, v'ha-ikar lo l'facheid k'lal.

The entire world is but a narrow bridge, but the most important thing is not to be afraid.

HAL'LUYAH IVDU AVDEI

הַלְלוּיָהּ עִבְדוּ עַבְדֵי יְיָ.

Hal'luyah ivdu avdei Adonai.

Praise the Eternal, you servants of God.

HARIU L'ADONAI

הָרִיעוּ לַיְיָ כָּל־הָאָרֶץ! פִּצְחוּ וְרַנְּנוּ וְזַמֵּרוּ.
כִּי־טוֹב יְיָ לְעוֹלָם חַסְדּוֹ.

Hariu l'Adonai kol haaretz! Pitzchu v'ran'nu v'zameiru.
Ki tov Adonai l'olam chasdo.

Shout joyfully to *Adonai*, all the earth! Break into song,
rejoice, and sing. For *Adonai* is good and God's love is
everlasting.

HAVAH NAGILAH

הָבָה נָגִילָה וְנִשְׂמְחָה, הָבָה נְרַנְּנָה וְנִשְׂמְחָה.
עוּרוּ אַחִים בְּלֵב שָׂמֵחַ.

Havah nagilah v'nism'chah, havah n'ran'nah v'nism'chah.
Uru achim b'lev samei-ach.

Come, let us be glad and rejoice. Let us sing.
Arise, friends, with a joyful heart.

HEIVEINU

הֵבֵאנוּ שָׁלוֹם עֲלֵיכֶם, עֲלֵיכֶם הֵבֵאנוּ שָׁלוֹם.
הִנֵּה מַה־טּוֹב וּמַה־נָּעִים שֶׁבֶת אַחִים גַּם יָחַד.

Heiveinu shalom aleichem, aleichem heiveinu shalom.
Hinei mah tov umah naim shevet achim gam yachad.

Peace unto you. How good and pleasant it is for everyone
to live together in peace.

HINEI MAH TOV

הִנֵּה מַה־טוֹב וּמַה־נָּעִים שֶׁבֶת אַחִים גַּם יָחַד.

Hinei mah tov umah naim shevet achim gam yachad.

How good and pleasant it is for everyone to live together in peace.

HODU L'ADONAI

הוֹדוּ לַיְיָ כִּי־טוֹב. כִּי לְעוֹלָם חַסְדּוֹ.

Hodu l'Adonai ki tov. Ki l'olam chasdo.

Give thanks to God, for God is good. God's mercy endures forever.

THE HOPE

This is the hope, the hope is still real
A Jewish home in Yisrael
This is the time we stand as one
If not now, when: We must be strong
Our hearts turn to the East.

CHORUS: This is the hope that holds us together
Hatikvah, the hope that will last forever
This is the hope that holds us together
Hatikvah, the hope is still real.

This is the hope, for 2,000 years
We pray for freedom through pain and tears
This is our faith, this is our voice
This is our promise, this is our choice

Our hearts turn to the East.
Hatikvah, the hope is real
Hatikvah, our home Israel

L'hiyot (L'hiyot) am chofshi (am chofshi)
b'artzeinu (b'artzeinu) b'artzeinu (b'artzeinu)
B'Eretz (B'Eretz) Tziyon (Tziyon)
Y'rushalayim (Y'rushalayim) Y'rushalayim (Y'rushalayim)

CHORUS

IM EIN ANI LI, MI LI?

אִם אֵין אֲנִי לִי מִי לִי, וּכְשֶׁאֲנִי לְעַצְמִי, מָה אֲנִי,
וְאִם לֹא עַכְשָׁו אֵימָתָי?

Im ein ani li mi li, uch'she-ani l'atzmi mah ani,
v'im lo achshav eimatai?

If I am not for myself, who will be for me? If I am only
for myself, what am I? And if not now, when?

IM TIRTZU

אִם תִּרְצוּ אֵין זוֹ אַגָּדָה לִהְיוֹת עַם
חָפְשִׁי בְּאַרְצֵנוּ בְּאֶרֶץ צִיּוֹן וִירוּשָׁלָיִם.

Im tirtzu ein zo aggadah lihyot am chofshi b'artzeinu
b'Eretz Tziyon Virushalayim.

If you will it, it is no legend to be a free people in our
land, in the land of Zion and Jerusalem.

IVDU ET HASHEM

עִבְדוּ אֶת־הַשֵּׁם בְּשִׂמְחָה, בֹּאוּ לְפָנָיו בִּרְנָנָה.

Ivdu et HaShem b'simchah, bo-u l'fanav birnanah.

Serve God with gladness! Come into God's presence
with singing.

K'HILAH K'DOSHAH

If you are *atem*, then we're *nitzavim*,
We stand here today and remember the dream.
If you are *atem*, then we're *nitzavim*,
We stand here today and remember the dream.

K'hilah k'doshah . . .

Yai lai lai . . .

Each one of us must play a part.
Each one of us must heed the call.
Each one of us must seek the truth.
Each one of us is a part of it all.
Each one of us must remember the pain.
Each one of us must find the joy.
Each one of us, each one of us.

K'hilah k'doshah . . .

Each one of us must start to hear.
Each one of us must sing the song.
Each one of us must do the work.
Each one of us must right the wrong.
Each one of us must build the home.

Each one of us must hold the hope.
Each one of us, each one of us.

K'hilah K'doshah . . .

It's how we help, it's how we give,
It's how we pray, it's how we heal, it's how we live.
(To beginning through ''Yai lai lai'')

KOL HAN'SHAMAH

כֹּל הַנְּשָׁמָה תְּהַלֵּל יָהּ. הַלְלוּיָהּ.

Kol han'shamah t'haleil Yah. Hal'luyah.

May everything that has breath praise God.
Praise be to God.

LO ALECHA

לֹא עָלֶיךָ הַמְּלָאכָה לִגְמֹר
וְלֹא אַתָּה בֶּן חוֹרִין לְהִבָּטֵל מִמֶּנָּה.

*Lo alecha ham'lachah ligmor
v'lo atah ben chorin l'hibateil mimenah.*

It is not your duty to complete the work, neither are you
free to desist from it.

LO YAREI-U

לֹא יָרֵעוּ וְלֹא יַשְׁחִיתוּ.
וְכִתְּתוּ חַרְבוֹתָם לְאִתִּים וַחֲנִיתוֹתֵיהֶם לְמַזְמֵרוֹת.
לֹא יִשָּׂא גוֹי אֶל גוֹי חֶרֶב, לֹא יִלְמְדוּ עוֹד מִלְחָמָה.

Lo yarei-u v'lo yashchitu.
V'chit'tu charvotam l'itim vachanitoteihem l'mazmeirot.
Lo yisa goi el goi cherev, lo yilm'du od milchamah.

They shall not hurt or destroy. They shall beat their
swords into plowshares, their spears into pruning-hooks.
Nation shall not lift up sword against nation, nor ever
again shall they train for war.

LO YISA GOI

לֹא יִשָּׂא גוֹי אֶל גוֹי חֶרֶב, לֹא יִלְמְדוּ עוֹד מִלְחָמָה.

Lo yisa goi el goi cherev, lo yilm'du od milchamah.

Nation shall not lift up sword against nation,
nor ever again shall they train for war.

L'TAKEIN (THE NA NA SONG)

בָּרוּךְ אַתָּה יְיָ אֱלֹהֵינוּ מֶלֶךְ הָעוֹלָם,
שֶׁנָּתַן לָנוּ הִזְדַּמְּנוּת לְתַקֵּן אֶת הָעוֹלָם.

Baruch atah Adonai Eloheinu Melech haolam,
shenatan lanu hizdam'nut l'takein et haolam.

We praise You, Eternal God, Ruler of the universe,
for giving us the opportunity to mend the world.

MILIBEINU

מִלִּבֵּנוּ אֲנַחְנוּ שָׁרִים וּבָחַרְתָּ בַּחַיִּים
וּבָחַרְתָּ בַּחַיִּים לְמַעַן תִּחְיֶה וּזְכֹר
כִּי בַּזְּכִירָה סוֹד גְּאֻלָּה מִלִּבֵּנוּ.

Milibeinu anachnu sharim uvacharta bachayim
uvacharta bachayim l'maan tichyeh uz'chor
ki baz'chirah sod g'ulah milibeinu.

From our heart we sing, "Therefore, choose life that you
may live," and remember, "For in remembrance is the
secret of redemption."

MIRIAM'S SONG

CHORUS: And the women dancing with their timbrels
Followed Miriam as she sang her song.
Sing a song to the One whom we've exalted.
Miriam and the women danced and danced the whole
    night long.

And Miriam was a weaver of unique variety,
The tapestry she wove was one which sang our history.
With every strand and every thread she crafted her delight,
A woman touched with spirit, as she dances toward
    the light.

CHORUS

When Miriam stood upon the shores and gazed across
    the sea,
The wonder of this miracle she soon came to believe.
Whoever thought the sea would part with an
    outstretched hand
And we would pass to freedom and march to the
    promised land?

CHORUS

And Miriam the prophet took her timbrel in her hand
And all the women followed her, just as she had planned.
And Miriam raised her voice in song, she sang with praise
    and might:
"We've just lived through a miracle; we're going to dance
    tonight."

CHORUS

MITZVAH GORERET MITZVAH

מִצְוָה גּוֹרֶרֶת מִצְוָה, עֲבֵרָה גּוֹרֶרֶת עֲבֵרָה.
לִהְיוֹת צַדִּיק זֶה טוֹב מְאֹד.

Mitzvah goreret mitzvah, aveirah goreret aveirah.
Lihyot tzadik zeh tov m'od.

One performed mitzvah leads to another. One sin leads
to another. To be righteous is very good.

NOT BY MIGHT—NOT BY POWER

Not by might and not by power
But by spirit alone shall we all live in peace.

The children sing, the children dream
And their tears may fall, but we'll hear them call
And another song will rise,
Another song will rise,
Another song will rise.

OR ZARUA

אוֹר זָרֻעַ לַצַּדִּיק וּלְיִשְׁרֵי לֵב שִׂמְחָה.

Or zarua latzadik ul'yishrei lev simchah.

Light is sown for the righteous and joy for the upright
in heart.

OSEH SHALOM

עֹשֶׂה שָׁלוֹם בִּמְרוֹמָיו, הוּא יַעֲשֶׂה שָׁלוֹם
עָלֵינוּ וְעַל כָּל־יִשְׂרָאֵל, וְאִמְרוּ: אָמֵן.

Oseh shalom bimromav, hu yaaseh shalom aleinu
v'al kol Yisrael, v'imru: Amen.

May the One who causes peace to reign in the high
heavens let peace descend on us and on all Israel,
and let us say: Amen.

PSALM 150

הַלְלוּיָהּ!
הַלְלוּ־אֵל בְּקָדְשׁוֹ, הַלְלוּהוּ בִּרְקִיעַ עֻזּוֹ,
הַלְלוּהוּ בִגְבוּרֹתָיו, הַלְלוּהוּ כְּרֹב גֻּדְלוֹ.
הַלְלוּהוּ בְּתֵקַע שׁוֹפָר, הַלְלוּהוּ בְּנֵבֶל וְכִנּוֹר,
הַלְלוּהוּ בְּתֹף וּמָחוֹל, הַלְלוּהוּ בְּמִנִּים וְעֻגָב.
הַלְלוּהוּ בְצִלְצְלֵי־שָׁמַע, הַלְלוּהוּ בְּצִלְצְלֵי־תְרוּעָה.
כֹּל הַנְּשָׁמָה תְּהַלֵּל יָהּ.
הַלְלוּיָהּ!

Hal'luyah! Hal'lu El b'kodsho, hal'luhu birkia uzo.
Hal'luhu bigvurotav, hal'luhu k'rov gudlo.
Hal'luhu b'teika shofar, hal'luhu b'neivel v'chinor.
Hal'luhu b'tof umachol, hal'luhu b'minim v'ugav.
Hal'luhu b'tziltz'lei shama, hal'luhu b'tziltz'lei t'ruah.
Kol han'shamah t'haleil Yah. Hal'luyah!

Hallelu-Yah! Praise God in the sanctuary; praise the
One whose power the heavens proclaim. Praise God for
mighty acts, praise the One for surpassing greatness.
Praise with shofar blast, praise with harp and lute,
praise with drum and dance, praise with strings and pipe,
praise with cymbals sounding, praise with cymbals
resounding! Let all that breathes praise God! Hallelu-Yah!

SHIR CHADASH

שִׁירוּ לַיְיָ כָּל־הָאָרֶץ, שִׁירוּ לַיְיָ שִׁיר חָדָשׁ.

Shiru l'Adonai kol haaretz, shiru l'Adonai shir chadash.

Sing unto God all the earth, sing unto God a new song.

SHIRU L'ADONAI

שִׁירוּ לַיְיָ שִׁיר חָדָשׁ. שִׁירוּ לַיְיָ כָּל־הָאָרֶץ.
שִׁירוּ לַיְיָ, בָּרְכוּ שְׁמוֹ, בַּשְּׂרוּ מִיּוֹם־לְיוֹם יְשׁוּעָתוֹ.

Shiru l'Adonai shir chadash. Shiru l'Adonai kol haaretz.
Shiru l'Adonai, bar'chu sh'mo, bas'ru miyom l'yom y'shuato.

Sing unto God a new song. Sing to God, all the earth.
Sing to God, bless God's name; tell of God's salvation
from day to day.

Sing unto God, all the earth, a new song
I will sing unto God a new song (*repeat*)

SHIRU SHIR

שִׁירוּ שִׁיר הַלְלוּיָהּ, שִׁירוּ שִׁיר חָדָשׁ לַיְיָ.

Shiru shir hal'luyah, shiru shir chadash l'Adonai.

Sing a song of praise to God. Sing unto God a new song.

V'EIZEHU

וְאֵיזֶהוּ חָכָם? הַלּוֹמֵד מִכָּל אָדָם.
וְאֵיזֶהוּ גִּבּוֹר? הַכּוֹבֵשׁ אֶת יִצְרוֹ.
וְאֵיזֶהוּ עָשִׁיר? הַשָּׂמֵחַ בְּחֶלְקוֹ.

V'eizehu chacham? Halomeid mikol adam.
V'eizehu gibor? Hakoveish et yitzro.
V'eizehu ashir? Hasamei-ach b'chelko.

Who is wise? Those who learn from all people. Who is
strong? Those who control their impulses. Who is rich?
Those who are happy with what they have.

WHEREVER YOU GO

Wherever you go there's always someone Jewish
You're never alone when you say you're a Jew.
So when you're not home and you're somewhere kind
    of "newish"
The odds are don't look far 'cause they're Jewish too.

Some Jews live in tents and some live in pagodas
And some Jews pay rent 'cause the city's not free.
Some Jews live on farms in the hills of Minnesota
And some Jews wear no shoes and sleep by the sea.

Amsterdam, Disneyland, Tel Aviv, oh, they're miles apart.
But when we light the candles on Sabbath Eve,
We share in the prayer in each one of our hearts.

And some Jews wear hats and some Jews wear sombreros
And some wear kaffiyehs to keep out the sun
Some Jews live on rice and some live on potatoes
Or waffles, falafels, or hamburger buns.

Amsterdam, Disneyland, Tel Aviv, oh, they're miles apart.
But when we light the candles on Sabbath eve,
We share in the prayer in each one of our hearts.

YAD B'YAD

יָד בְּיָד אֶחָד עִם הַשֵּׁנִי. עַם אֶחָד עִם לֵב אֶחָד
כֵּן אָנוּ נַדְלִיק. נַדְלִיק מַשּׂוּאַת עוֹלָם
נַדְלִיקָה כְּעַם אֶחָד. יָד בְּיָד אֶחָד כֵּן אָנוּ נַדְלִיק.
אִם אֵין קֶמַח אֵין תּוֹרָה, אִם אֵין תּוֹרָה אֵין קֶמַח.

Yad b'yad echad im hasheini.
Am echad im lev echad kein anu nadlik.
Nadlik masuat olam nadlikah k'am echad.
Yad b'yad echad echad kein anu nadlik.
Im ein kemach ein Torah, im ein Torah ein kemach.

Hand in hand, one with the other, one people with one
heart, we will light. We will light a torch for the world,
it will be lit as one people. Hand in hand, one by one,
we will light.
If there is no sustenance, there is no Torah; if no Torah,
no sustenance.

It can be you, it can be me, it can be all people all over the
world
Lending, caring, sharing hand in hand (*repeat*)

YISM'CHU HASHAMAYIM

יִשְׂמְחוּ הַשָּׁמַיִם וְתָגֵל הָאָרֶץ!
יִרְעַם הַיָּם וּמְלֹאוֹ!

Yism'chu hashamayim v'tageil haaretz!
Yiram hayam um'lo-o!

Let the heavens be glad! Let the earth rejoice,
let the sea roar and all that fills it!

ANTHEMS

HATIKVAH—ISRAELI NATIONAL ANTHEM

כָּל עוֹד בַּלֵּבָב פְּנִימָה נֶפֶשׁ יְהוּדִי הוֹמִיָּה
וּלְפַאֲתֵי מִזְרָח קָדִימָה עַיִן לְצִיּוֹן צוֹפִיָּה
עוֹד לֹא אָבְדָה תִּקְוָתֵנוּ הַתִּקְוָה (בַּת) שְׁנוֹת אַלְפַּיִם
לִהְיוֹת עַם חָפְשִׁי בְּאַרְצֵנוּ אֶרֶץ צִיּוֹן וִירוּשָׁלַיִם.

Kol od baleivav p'nimah nefesh Y'hudi homiyah
Ul'faatei mizrach kadimah ayin l'Tziyon tzofiyah
Od lo av'dah tikvateinu hatikvah (bat) sh'not alpayim
Lihyot am chofshi b'artzeinu Eretz Tziyon Virushalayim.

So long as still within the inmost a Jewish spirit sings,
so long as the eye looks eastward, gazing toward Zion,
our hope is not lost—the hope of two thousand years:
to be a free people in our land, the land of Zion and
Jerusalem.

THE STAR-SPANGLED BANNER—
U.S. NATIONAL ANTHEM

Oh say, can you see, by the dawn's early light,
What so proudly we hailed at the twilight's last gleaming?
Whose broad stripes and bright stars, through the perilous
    fight,
O'er the ramparts we watched, were so gallantly streaming?
And the rockets' red glare, the bombs bursting in air,
Gave proof through the night that our flag was still there.
Oh say, does that star-spangled banner yet wave
O'er the land of the free and the home of the brave?

O CANADA—CANADIAN NATIONAL ANTHEM

O Canada!
Our home and native land!
True patriot love in all thy sons command.

With glowing hearts we see thee rise,
The True North strong and free!

From far and wide,
O Canada, we stand on guard for thee.

God keep our land glorious and free!
O Canada, we stand on guard for thee.

O Canada, we stand on guard for thee.

BLESSINGS

Shalom Aleichem, from *Mishkan T'filah* (CCAR Press)

Lighting Shabbat Candles, from *Mishkan T'filah* (CCAR Press)

Blessings for Loved Ones, from *Mishkan T'filah* (CCAR Press)

Reading before *Kiddush* for Shabbat Evening, from *On the Doorposts of Your House* (CCAR Press)

Kiddush for Shabbat Evening, from *Mishkan T'filah* (CCAR Press)

Blessing for Challah, from *Mishkan T'filah* (CCAR Press)

Birkat HaMazon, short version, from *Mishkan T'filah* (CCAR Press)

Birkat HaMazon, long version, adapted from *On the Doorposts of Your House* (CCAR Press)

Kiddush for Shabbat Morning, *Mishkan T'filah* (CCAR Press)

Havdalah, from *Mishkan T'filah* (CCAR Press)

Lighting Holiday Candles, from *Mishkan T'filah* (CCAR Press)

Kiddush for Holidays, from *Mishkan T'filah* (CCAR Press)

Lighting the Chanukah Candles, from *Mishkan T'filah* (CCAR Press)

Blessings for Sukkot, from *On the Doorposts of Your House* (CCAR Press) and from *Mishkan T'filah* (CCAR Press)

Lighting a *Yahrzeit* (Memorial) Candle, "O God, grant us . . .": Kerry M. Olitzky and Ronald H. Isaacs, *The How-To Handbook for Jewish Living*, Ktav, 1993, p. 97.

Eating Bread, from *Mishkan T'filah* (CCAR Press)

Eating Food Prepared from Grain (other than bread), from *Mishkan T'filah* (CCAR Press)

Drinking Wine/Grape Juice, from *On the Doorposts of Your House* (CCAR Press)

Eating Fruit, from *On the Doorposts of Your House* (CCAR Press)

Eating Food that Grows from the Ground, from *On the Doorposts of Your House* (CCAR Press)

All Other Food and Drink, from *On the Doorposts of Your House* (CCAR Press)

Sheva B'rachot, from *On the Doorposts of Your House* (CCAR Press)

Thanksgiving for Other Food, from *On the Doorposts of Your House* (CCAR Press)

SONGS

For Shabbat

Bo-i Kalah: Shlomo Alkabetz (16th c.)

Dodi Li: Song of Songs 2:16, 3:6, 4:9, 4:16

D'ror Yikra: Dunash HaLevi ben Labrat (10th c.)

Eileh Cham'dah Libi: Chasidic folk song

Eit Dodim: Based on Song of Songs 6:11

HaRachaman: Birkat HaMazon

Ki Eshm'rah Shabbat: Abraham ibn Ezra

L'chu N'ran'nah: Psalm 95:1

Mah Yafeh Hayom: Isaachar Miron; text: unknown

Mizmor Shir: Psalm 92:1–4

Od Yishama: Jeremiah 33:10–11

Rom'mu: Psalm 99:9

Shir Hamaalot: Psalm 126:1–2

Tzadik Katamar: Psalm 92:13–16

V'taheir Libeinu: Liturgy

Y'did Nefesh: Liturgy

Yom Zeh L'Yisrael: Isaac Luria (16th c.)

For Every Day

Adonai Oz: Psalm 29:11

Am Yisrael Chai: Unknown

Ani V'atah: © by Composers/ACUM, Ltd.
    Lyrics by Arik Einstein.

Ashrei: Psalms 84:5, 144:15

BaShanah HaBaah: © by Composers/ACUM, Ltd.
    Text: Ehud Manor.

BaYom HaHu: Zechariah 14:9

B'Makom: Pirkei Avot 2:5

B'Tzelem Elohim: © 2001 by Dan Nichols.
    Lyrics by Dan Nichols and Mike Moskowitz.

Eitz Chayim Hi: Proverbs 3:18

Gesher Tzar M'od: Rabbi Nachman of Bratzlav

Hal'luyah Ivdu Avdei: Based on Psalm 113:1

Hariu L'Adonai: Psalms 98:4, 100:5

Havah Nagilah: Moshe Nathanson

Heiveinu: Folk song, Psalm 133:1

Hinei Mah Tov: Psalm 133:1

Hodu L'Adonai: Psalm 118:1

The Hope: © 2003 by Rick Recht (ASCAP).
    Lyrics by Rick Recht and N. H. Imber.

Im Ein Ani Li Mi Li? *Pirkei Avot* 1:14

Im Tirtzu: Theodor Hertzl, Naftali Imber

Ivdu Et HaShem: Psalm 100:2

K'hilah K'doshah: © 2002 by Dan Nichols.
    Lyrics by Dan Nichols and Mike Moskowitz.

Kol HaN'shamah: Psalm 150:6

Lo Alecha: *Pirkei Avot* 2:16, 2:15

Lo Yarei-u: Isaiah 11:9, 2:4

Lo Yisa Goi: Isaiah 2:4

L'takein (The Na Na Song): © 2001 by Dan Nichols.
    Lyrics by Ron Klotz.

Milibeinu: Deuteronomy 30:19, Baal Shem Tov

Miriam's Song: © 1988 by Deborah Lynn Friedman
    (ASCAP) / Sounds Write Productions (ASCAP). Lyrics
    by Debbie Friedman based on Exodus 15:20–21.
    www.debbiefriedman.com and www.soundswrite.com

Mitzvah Goreret Mitzvah: *Pirkei Avot* 4:2, Andy Vogel